Fit fürs Gymnasium

Englisch

Schroedel

Fit fürs **Gymnasium**

Englisch

Autorin:
Julia Käufler ist Lehrerin für Deutsch und Englisch an einem bayerischen Gymnasium. Zudem unterrichtet sie Englisch im Kindergarten und arbeitet mit Grundschulkindern. Daher kennt sie die Schwierigkeiten, die beim Übertritt von der Grundschule ans Gymnasium im Fach Englisch auftreten können.

Unter Mitarbeit von Christina Hofmeier und Sonja von der Heyde.

Druck [1] / Jahr 2015

Redaktion: imprint, Zusmarshausen
Umschlaggestaltung und Layout: Janssen Kahlert Design & Kommunikation GmbH, Hannover
Umschlagfoto: Corbis, Berlin
Illustrationen: Hans-Jürgen Feldhaus, Münster
Druck und Bindung: westermann druck GmbH, Braunschweig

ISBN 978-3-507-**23271**-6

Vorwort

Liebe Schülerin, lieber Schüler,

du stehst kurz vor dem Übergang in die 5. Klasse des Gymnasiums? *Fit fürs Gymnasium* hilft dir, deine Leistungen im Fach Englisch richtig einzuordnen und das zu trainieren, was du noch nicht sicher genug beherrschst. Wie arbeitest du mit diesem Buch?

1. Beginne mit dem Einstiegstest. Bearbeite jeweils einen Teilbereich (A bis E). Für einen Teilbereich benötigst du ungefähr 45 Minuten.
2. Mithilfe der Lösungen im Anhang kontrollierst du, ob du die Test-Aufgaben richtig bearbeitet hast.
   Notiere deine Ergebnisse im Lernplaner (auf Seite 6).
3. Der Lernplaner gibt dir eine Übersicht darüber, welche Themen dir noch Schwierigkeiten bereiten und welche Kapitel du daher als Erstes bearbeiten solltest. Am Ende jedes Kapitels kannst du mithilfe des Zwischentests deinen Lernfortschritt überprüfen.
4. Nachdem du alle Kapitel durchgearbeitet hast, in denen du noch Schwierigkeiten hattest, bist du fit für den Abschlusstest.

Alle Übungen, zu denen es Audio-Dateien gibt, erkennst du am QR-Code und am links abgebildeten Symbol. Scanne den Code mit einem Handy oder Tablet, dann gelangst du zu dem jeweiligen Hörtext. Alle Hörtexte findest du auch unter **www.schroedel.de/Uebergang-Gymnasium**

Wenn du im Buch nicht genügend Platz zur Bearbeitung der Aufgaben findest, nimm einfach ein Heft zur Hand.

Viel Erfolg beim Üben mit *Fit fürs Gymnasium*!
Julia Käufler

Eltern-Spezial

Liebe Eltern,

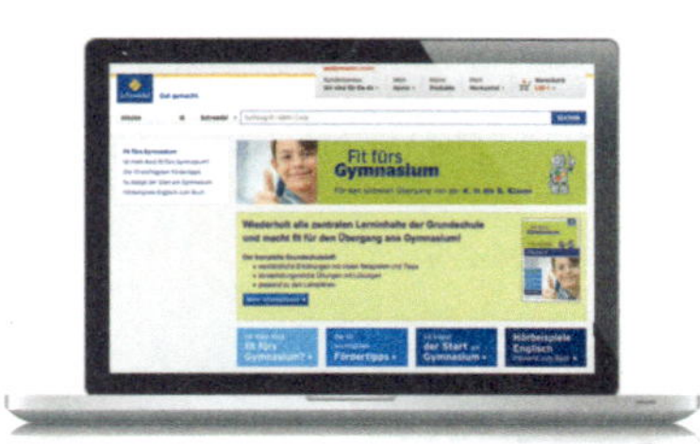

wie Sie Ihre Kinder auf dem Weg ins Gymnasium am besten unterstützen, erfahren Sie auf:
www.schroedel.de/Uebergang-Gymnasium

Auf dieser Website haben wir praktische Checklisten und Fördertipps für Sie zusammengestellt.

Inhalt

Lernplaner

1. Bearbeite den Einstiegstest. Kreuze hier an, welches Ergebnis du in den verschiedenen Teilbereichen erzielt hast.

Teilbereich Einstiegstest				Seiten im Buch
A At school				Seite 12 bis 20
B My wardrobe/Body and feelings				Seite 21 bis 34
C My family/At home/ Food and time				Seite 35 bis 66
D Nature/My free time				Seite 67 bis 86
E The year				Seite 87 bis 95

2. Bei welchen Teilbereichen hast du  angekreuzt?
Notiere sie in der Tabelle unten. Beginne mit dem schlechtesten Ergebnis.
Bearbeite dann die angegebenen Seiten im Buch der Reihe nach.
Dein Ergebnis im Zwischentest sollte nun mindestens ein  sein.

Teilbereich Einstiegstest	Ergebnis Einstiegs-test	erledigen bis	Ergebnis Zwischen-test

3. Ergänze, wo du im Einstiegstest ein  erreicht hast. In diesen Bereichen bereiten dir wahrscheinlich nur bestimmte Aufgabentypen Schwierigkeiten. Konzentriere dich darauf, wenn du das jeweilige Kapitel bearbeitest.
Auch wenn du überwiegend  erzielt hast, kannst du dieses Buch nutzen, um noch sicherer zu werden.

4. Kontrolliere deinen Lernerfolg mithilfe des Abschlusstests.

Einstiegstest

A At school

1 Write sentences.
Schreibe jeweils einen Satz auf die Zeilen.

This *is a ruler.* ....

a) This ....

b) Is .... ?

c) ....

maximale Punktzahl 3

2 Write down the numbers. – Schreibe die Zahlen darunter.

18 ....

23 ....

89 ....

34 ....

maximale Punktzahl 4

3 Connect the sentences with the same meaning.
Verbinde die Sätze, die dasselbe bedeuten.

A	*Open your exercise book, please!*
B	*How are you?*
C	*What's … in English/German?*
D	*Repeat the word/sentence!*
E	*Take out your ruler!*
F	*Sit down, please!*

1	Wie geht es Ihnen?
2	Schlage bitte dein Heft auf.
3	Wiederhole das Wort/den Satz!
4	Was heißt … auf Englisch/Deutsch?
5	Setzt euch, bitte!
6	Nimm dein Lineal heraus!

maximale Punktzahl 6

Kontrolliere deine Ergebnisse mithilfe der Lösungen (Seite 101) und addiere die erreichten Punkte.

Teilbereich A: ☐ 13 bis 11 Punkte: ☐ 10 bis 8 Punkte: ☐ 7 bis 0 Punkte:

Lernplaner

Gesamtpunktzahl .... von 13

Einstiegstest

B My wardrobe / Body and feelings

4 **Write down the colour. – Schreibe die Farbe auf die Linie.**

maximale Punktzahl 3

 ....  ....  ....

5 **Can you answer the question? – Kannst du die Fragen beantworten?**

maximale Punktzahl 3

a) Is Stefanie's sweatshirt orange? Yes, it is.

b) Are her shoes blue and white? ....

c) Are her trousers blue? ....

d) Are the socks blue, too? No, they aren't.

e) Is her sweatshirt green? ....

6 **Fill in the gaps. – Vervollständige die Sätze.**

maximale Punktzahl 5

ten years • name • 2843 • orange • London

Hello, my .... is Stefanie.

I'm .... old.

My favourite colour is ....

My telephone number is ....

I live in ....

7 **Tick the right answer. – Kreuze die richtige Antwort an.**

maximale Punktzahl 2

a) 

- ☐ She is sad.
- ☐ She is happy.
- ☐ She is tired.

b) 

- ☐ He is happy.
- ☐ He is hungry.
- ☐ He is thirsty.

Gesamtpunktzahl .... von 13

Lernplaner

Kontrolliere deine Ergebnisse mithilfe der Lösungen (Seite 101) und addiere die erreichten Punkte.

Teilbereich B: ☐ 13 bis 11 Punkte: ☐ 10 bis 7 Punkte: ☐ 6 bis 0 Punkte:

Einstiegstest

C My family / At home / Food

8 Tick the right answer. – Kreuze die richtige Antwort an.

a) My mother's mother is my
- ☐ grandparents.
- ☐ grandmother.
- ☐ aunt.

b) When is Oliver's birthday?
- ☐ His birthday is in April.
- ☐ Her birthday is in April.
- ☐ He is birthday in April.

maximale Punktzahl 2

9 There are eight "house words". Write them down.
Hier sind acht Wörter zum Thema „Haus". Schreibe Sie auf.

D	S	C	O	R	C
O	E	I	J	K	A
O	O	S	J	Y	R
R	W	T	K	H	P
G	A	R	A	G	E
I	L	L	S	Z	T
F	L	O	O	R	U
W	I	N	D	O	W
U	C	H	A	I	R

....
....
....
....
....
....
....
....

maximale Punktzahl 8

10 Answer the questions. – Beantworte die Fragen.

Do you like cornflakes with milk for breakfast?

☺ Yes, ...

Do you like toast with cheese for dinner?

☹ ....

maximale Punktzahl 2

11 What time is it? Make sentences. – Wie spät ist es? Bilde Sätze.

a)

It's ....

b)

....

maximale Punktzahl 2

Kontrolliere deine Ergebnisse mithilfe der Lösungen (Seite 101) und addiere die erreichten Punkte.

Teilbereich C: ☐ 14 bis 11 Punkte: ☺ ☐ 10 bis 7 Punkte: 😐 ☐ 6 bis 0 Punkte: ☹

Lernplaner

Gesamtpunktzahl
.... von 14

Einstiegstest

D Nature / My free time

12 **What do you see? Make sentences. – Was siehst du? Bilde Sätze.**

a) 
b) 
c) 
d) 

a) This is a ....

b) These are two ....

c) This ....

d) These are ....

maximale Punktzahl 4

13 **Make sentences. – Bilde Sätze.**

In sunny hot it is Dublin and . 	....
In foggy it is and cold Cambridge. 	....

maximale Punktzahl 4

14 **What is right? Tick it. – Was ist richtig?**

a) They
- ☐ am playing tennis.
- ☐ is playing tennis.
- ☐ are playing tennis.

b) He
- ☐ am riding his bike.
- ☐ is climbing.
- ☐ are skiing.

maximale Punktzahl 2

Gesamtpunktzahl
.... von 10

Lernplaner

Kontrolliere deine Ergebnisse mithilfe der Lösungen (Seite 101) und addiere die erreichten Punkte.

Teilbereich D: ☐ 10 bis 8 Punkte: ☐ 7 bis 5 Punkte: ☐ 4 bis 0 Punkte:

Einstiegstest

E The year

15 **What belongs together? Connect it.**
Was gehört zusammen? Verbinde.

Easter

Halloween

Christmas

gsoth ....

rdeirene ....

lmab ....

maximale Punktzahl 6

16 **Look at the pictures and complete the sentences.**
Schau dir die Bilder an und vervollständige die Sätze.

every Tuesday	every Thursday	every Friday

a) On Tuesdays I play ....

b) On ....

c) ....

maximale Punktzahl 5

17 **Write down the missing days. – Trage die fehlenden Wochentage ein.**

the day before	today	the day after
....	Tuesday	....
Friday	....	....

maximale Punktzahl 4

Kontrolliere deine Ergebnisse mithilfe der Lösungen (Seite 101) und addiere die erreichten Punkte.

Teilbereich E: ☐ 15 bis 12 Punkte: ☐ 11 bis 8 Punkte: ☐ 7 bis 0 Punkte:

Lernplaner

Gesamtpunktzahl .... von 15

At school

Das lernst du hier:

→ Wörter und Sätze, die du für die Schule brauchst.

→ Was es mit den Zahlen auf sich hat, und wie du sagen kannst, wie viel von etwas vorhanden ist.

In my classroom

REGEL

Im Englischen schreibt man auch Namenwörter klein.

1 What's this in English?

Write down the correct word from the box.

Wie heißen diese Dinge auf Englisch?

Schreibe das passende Wort aus dem Kästchen unter das Bild.

book, board, pen, desk, ruler, pencil case, chair, workbook, eraser, pencil

1. ....

2. ....

3. ....

4. ....

5. ....

6. ....

7. ....

8. ....

9. ....

10. ....

REGEL

this / that

This wird gebraucht, um auf Personen oder Dinge hinzuweisen, die in der Nähe sind, **that** auf solche, die sich weiter weg befinden.

Möchte man zwei Dinge oder Personen vorstellen, sagt man zuerst **this**, dann **that**.

"Look, mum! **This** is my new friend Peter and **that's** his sister Sarah."

"**This** is my schoolbag and **that's** my desk."

"I like **this** boy, but **that** one over there is really nasty*."

This classroom (here) is very small.

That classroom (there) is really big.

* nasty = böse, gemein

2 **Do you know this in English?**
Complete the questions and the answers.
Kennst du das auf Englisch? Ergänze die Fragen und Antworten.

What's this? 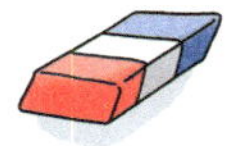 It's an ....

What's that?  It's a ....

What's .... 

....

....  ....

....  ....

....  ....

....  ....

....  ....

1

3 **Listen and find the objects which aren't mentioned.**
Höre gut zu und finde die Objekte, die nicht genannt werden.

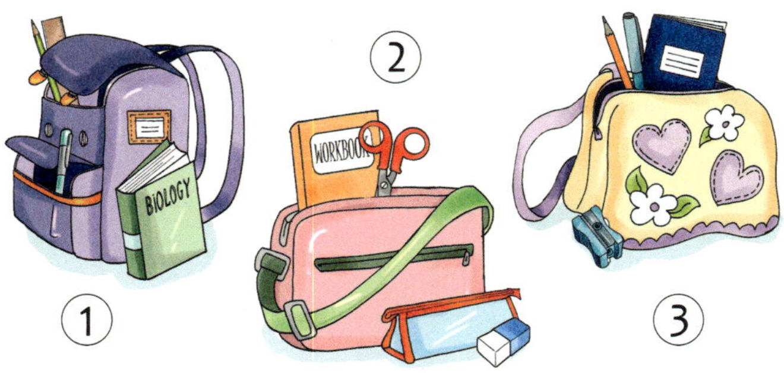

4 What's this?

a) Complete the question and find the correct answer.
Vervollständige die Frage und finde die richtige Antwort.

Is this ……………………………… ?  Yes, ……………………………… .

Is this ……………………………… ?  No, ……………………………… .

Is ……………………………… ?  No, ……………………………… .

b) Now draw your own picture and complete the sentences.
Male jetzt dein eigenes Bild und vervollständige die Sätze.

Is this a pencil? No, ……………………………… .
It's a ……………………………… .

5 In my English course

a) Read the text about form 4a. – Lies den Text über Klasse 4a.

Hello! We are form 4a. There are 16 boys and 13 girls. Our school is in Berlin. We can all speak English and German, of course! Our English teacher is Mrs Smith. Her favourite colour is red.

b) Compare form 4a with your own form and write a short text in your exercise book.
Vergleiche Klasse 4a mit deiner eigenen Klasse und schreibe einen kurzen Text darüber in dein Heft.

Numbers

one two three four five six seven eight nine ten

eleven twelve thirteen fourteen fifteen

sixteen seventeen eighteen nineteen twenty

twenty-one twenty-two twenty-three twenty-four twenty-five

thirty forty fifty sixty

seventy eighty ninety a/one hundred

6 Fill in the gaps. The letters will help you.
Vervollständige die Sätze. Die Buchstaben helfen dir dabei.

Bob is ......eleven...... . (l v n e e e)

Julia is .... (neetfruo)

Tom is .... (eetenihg)

Bob's dog is .... (vfie)

Julia's cat is .... (ent)

Tom's dog is .... (reeht)

My grandmother is .... (tynine)

There are (ifevtwnety) .... pupils in my class.

TIPP

five und twentyfive, aber fifteen und fifty

7 How much is this? Calculate.
Wie viel ergibt das? Rechne aus.

a) three + eight = ...

b) five + seven = ...

c) eleven + ten = ...

d) fifty-seven + forty-three = ...

e) eighteen – twelve = ...

twenty-one, fourteen, six, eleven, twenty-three, seven, one hundred, twelve

8 Write the numbers.
Schreibe die Zahlen auf.

TIPP

Höre dir an, wie im Englischen **Plus (+)** und **Minus (–)** in einer Rechenaufgabe gesprochen werden.

2

1 7 8 12 13 15 20 22

31 43 56 61 79 83 90 100

....

....

....

....

9 Look at the telephone numbers and listen. What numbers are called? Circle them. – Sieh dir die Telefonnummern an und höre gut zu. Welche Nummern werden genannt? Kreise sie ein.

3

555-3489 2649876 9873462

919823 349812 753417

10 Listen and fill in the boxes.
Höre gut zu und fülle die Kästchen aus.

4

11 Count the school objects and complete the senteces.
Zähle die Schulsachen und vervollständige die Sätze.

pencils • pens • rulers • erasers • sharpeners • books

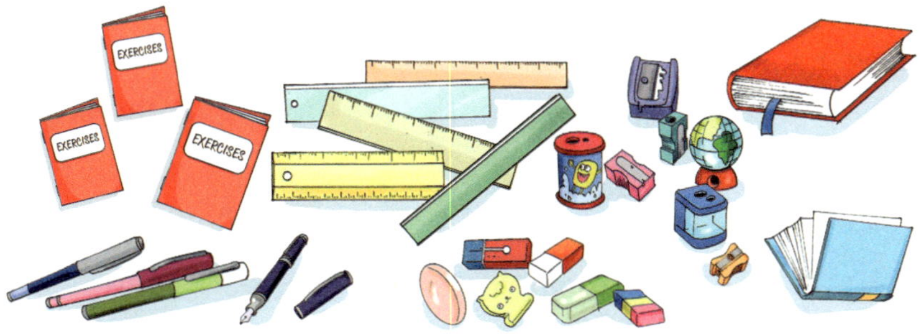

There are .... exercise books.

There are ....

There are .... There are ....

There are ....

5

12 Listen and connect the numbers in the right order.
Höre gut zu und verbinde die Nummern in der genannten Reihenfolge.

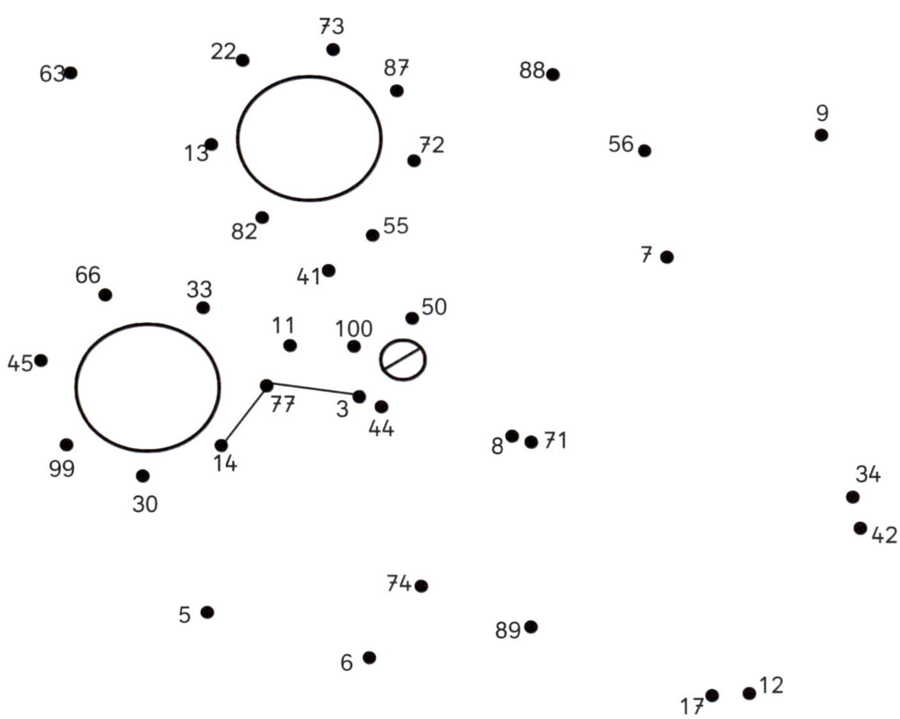

Classroom language

13 **Here are some important phrases that you can use in the classroom. Connect the English sentences with their German translation.**
Hier sind einige wichtige Formulierungen, die du im Klassenzimmer gebrauchen kannst. Verbinde die englischen Sätze jeweils mit ihrer deutschen Entsprechung.

A *Good morning.*	1 Wie geht es dir?
B *How are you?*	2 Guten Morgen.
C *What's … in English / German?*	3 Schlage bitte dein Heft auf.
D *Open your exercise book, please!*	4 Was heißt … auf Englisch / Deutsch?
E *Take out your ruler!*	5 Sei bitte still!
F *Please be quiet!*	6 Nimm dein Lineal heraus!
G *Sit down, please!*	7 Darf ich bitte auf die Toilette gehen?
H *May I go to the toilet, please?*	8 Setzt euch, bitte!
I *Repeat the word /sentence!*	9 Auf Wiedersehen.
J Goodbye.	10 Wiederhole das Wort / den Satz!
K *It's my turn.*	11 Hör(t) zu!
L *Listen!*	12 Ich bin dran.
M *Is this right / OK?*	13 Ich verstehe (das) nicht.
N *I don't understand.*	14 Ist das richtig / ok?
O *Can you say it again, please?*	15 Können Sie das bitte noch einmal sagen?

Zwischentest

1 Tick the correct word. – Kreuze das richtige Wort an.

a) 

- ☐ pencil
- ☐ ruler
- ☐ eraser

b) 

- ☐ sharpener
- ☐ exercise book
- ☐ glue

c) 

- ☐ book
- ☐ pen
- ☐ exercise book

d) 

- ☐ board
- ☐ chair
- ☐ table

e) 

- ☐ aight
- ☐ eight
- ☐ eith

f) 

- ☐ eleven
- ☐ elewen
- ☐ ilewen

g) 

- ☐ thirty
- ☐ thirteen
- ☐ three

h) 

- ☐ fifteen
- ☐ fifty
- ☐ fifty-two

i) 

- ☐ seventy
- ☐ eighty
- ☐ ninety

j) 

- ☐ threa
- ☐ tree
- ☐ three

Gesamtpunktzahl
.... von 10

Lernplaner

Kontrolliere deine Ergebnisse mithilfe der Lösungen (Seite 102) und addiere die erreichten Punkte.

☐ 10 bis 8 Punkte: ☐ 7 bis 5 Punkte: ☐ 4 bis 0 Punkte:

My wardrobe

Das lernst du hier:

- → Welche Farben dich umgeben.
- → Was du alles in deinem Kleiderschrank findest.
- → Was es mit dem Genitiv (2. Fall: „Wessen?“) auf sich hat.

Colours

1 **First colour the pots with the right colour and then write a sentence.**
Male die Farbtöpfe zuerst in der richtigen Farbe an und schreibe dann einen passenden Satz dazu.

I'm .... | .... | .... | .... | ....

.... | pink .... | .... | .... | ....

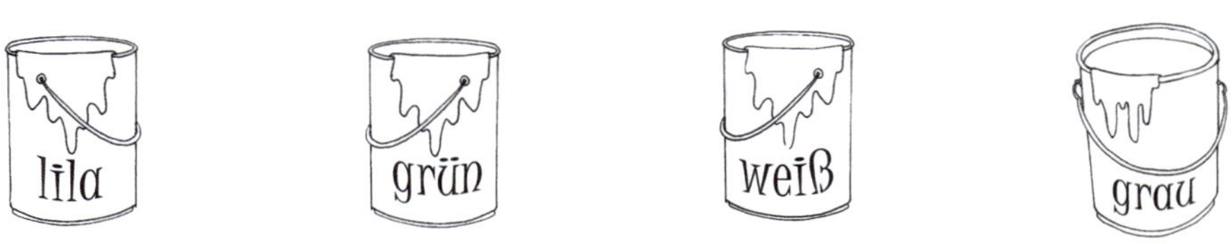

.... | .... | .... | ....

.... | .... | .... | ....

6

2 **Whose balloons are these? Listen and write down the children's names. – Wem gehören die Ballons? Höre gut zu und schreibe die Namen der Kinder auf die Zeilen.**

7

3 **Listen again and fill in the gaps.**
Höre dir die Aufnahme noch einmal an und vervollständige die Sätze.

_____'s balloon is ___ (2).

____'s balloon is ______ (5, 6).

Bob's balloon is ______ (1).

____'s balloon is _____ (3).

Betty's balloon is ____ (4).

Where are the children? They are at a H _ _ _ o _ ee _ p _ _ t _.

8

4 **Listen and tick the right answers.**
Höre zu und kreuze die richtigen Antworten an.

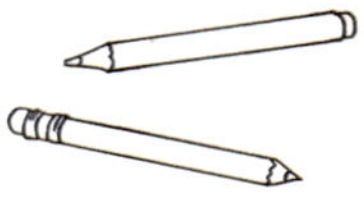

a) John's pencils are
- ☐ blue.
- ☐ green.
- ☐ red.

b) Betty's book is
- ☐ black.
- ☐ red.
- ☐ grey.

c) Peter's dog is
- ☐ black.
- ☐ brown.
- ☐ white.

Clothes

TIPP

Vielleicht kennst du folgende **Vokabeln** noch nicht:
vest – Unterhemd; *belt* – Gürtel; *(under-)pants* – Unterhose;
scarf – Schal.
Weil eine Hose zwei Beine hat, verwenden Englischsprechende immer die **Mehrzahl**, wenn sie von einer Hose sprechen: *trousers, pants, shorts.*

5 Read the text and connect the words with the objects in the picture.
Lies den Text und verbinde die Wörter mit den Kleidungsstücken im Bild.

This is Sarah in her room. She has a lot of clothes.
Sarah's jacket is green and blue. Her boots are blue and yellow.
Her skirt is green and her socks are grey. Her shoes are grey and red.
Her two pants are white and the vest is white, too.
And her pullover is green and red.
The dress is very nice. It is yellow and pink.
The belt is black and the scarf is blue and red.
And her warm jumper is brown and pink.
Her T-shirt is pink with a red heart ♥. And her trousers are pink, too.

belt • skirt • dress • T-shirt • boots • vest • jacket • trousers

shoes • scarf • pullovers • socks • pants

6 Children's clothes

a) Listen and find out the right colours for the clothes.
Then, complete the sentences and colour the clothes.
Höre zu und finde die Farben der Kleidungsstücke heraus.
Ergänze dann die Sätze und male die Kleidungsstücke in der richtigen Farbe an.

This is my .... T-shirt.

These trousers are very big. They are ....

This skirt is nice.

It is .... and ....

This pullover is too big. It is my brother's pullover.

It is .... and ....

b) Now, listen again and speak the sentences with the recording.
Höre die Aufnahme jetzt noch einmal an und sprich die Sätze mit.

7 Copy the chart in your exercise book and put the words in the right column. – Übertrage die Tabelle in dein Heft und ordne die Wörter in die richtigen Spalten ein.

~~nose~~ • eraser • red • blue • shirt • ruler • pullover • finger • ear • book • black • desk • trousers • grey • T-shirt • board • yellow • jeans • knee • purple • pink • skirt • foot • eye • toe • pencil • white • socks • arm • workbook • jacket

parts of the body (Körperteile)

clothes (Kleidungs-stücke)

school things (Schulsachen)

colours (Farben)

parts of the body	clothes	school things	colours
nose			

8 Who is Susan? Who is Julia?

Listen to the recording and tick the correct picture.
Wer ist Susan? Wer ist Julia? Höre zu und kreuze das richtige Bild an.

10

 ☐
 ☐
 ☐
 ☐

 ☐
 ☐
 ☐
 ☐

9 Susan and Julia

a) Look at Susan and Julia. What are they wearing? Fill in the gaps.
Schau dir Susan und Julia an. Was tragen sie? Vervollständige die Sätze.

Susan's jacket is .... and ....

Susan's .... aren't green, they are grey.

.... is brown and

her ....

Julia's .... is pink with a .... heart.

.... blue. .... aren't

red, they are grey. The girls' .... are blue.

b) Listen again and correct your sentences.
Höre die Aufnahme noch einmal an und korrigiere deine Sätze.

10

REGEL

s-Genitiv = Besitzfall

Die Aussprache ist wie beim Plural-s.

Einzahl: Hier machst du den **Apostroph vor dem s**: *Betty's.*

Mehrzahl: Hier machst du den **Apostroph nach dem Mehrzahl-s** und verzichtest auf ein weiteres **s**, da man das nicht aussprechen könnte: *girls'.*

10 **Write down who these things belong to.**
Schreibe auf, wem die abgebildeten Sachen gehören.
Start with: "This is …" or "These are …".

1. This is Betty's book.
2. This is ……………………
3. These are the girls' shoes.
4. ……………………
5. ……………………
6. ……………………
7. ……………………
8. ……………………

Zwischentest

1 Tick the right answer. – Kreuze die richtige Antwort an.

a) An elephant is
- ☐ blue.
- ☐ grey.
- ☐ green.

b) The ocean is
- ☐ blue.
- ☐ orange.
- ☐ white.

c) A zebra is
- ☐ black and yellow.
- ☐ orange and white.
- ☐ black and white.

d) My dog is
- ☐ blue.
- ☐ green.
- ☐ brown.

e)
- ☐ This is a scarf.
- ☐ This is a belt.
- ☐ These are pants.

f)
- ☐ This is a shoe.
- ☐ These are boots.
- ☐ These are socks.

g)
- ☐ This is a pullover.
- ☐ This is a jacket.
- ☐ This is a vest.

h)
- ☐ This is a green dress.
- ☐ This is a green skirt.
- ☐ This is a grey dress.

i)
- ☐ This is Bettys belt.
- ☐ This is Betty's belt.
- ☐ This is Bettys' belt.

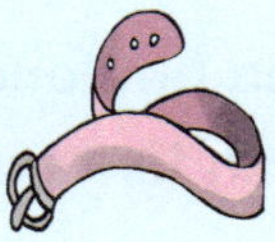

j)
- ☐ These is the girl's shoes.
- ☐ This is a girl's shoe.
- ☐ These are the girls' shoes.

Kontrolliere deine Ergebnisse mithilfe der Lösungen (Seite 103) und addiere die erreichten Punkte.

☐ 10 bis 8 Punkte: ☐ 7 bis 5 Punkte: ☐ 4 bis 0 Punkte:

Gesamtpunktzahl

.... von 10

Body and feelings

Das lernst du hier:

- → Wie du dich selbst beschreibst.
- → Wie du andere beschreiben kannst.
- → Wie du jemanden fragst, wie es ihm geht, und wie du selbst sagen kannst, wie es dir geht.

This is me

1 **What parts of the body do you know?**
Make a mind map in your exercise book.
Welche Körperteile kennst du?
Zeichne eine Mindmap (Wörternetz) in dein Heft.

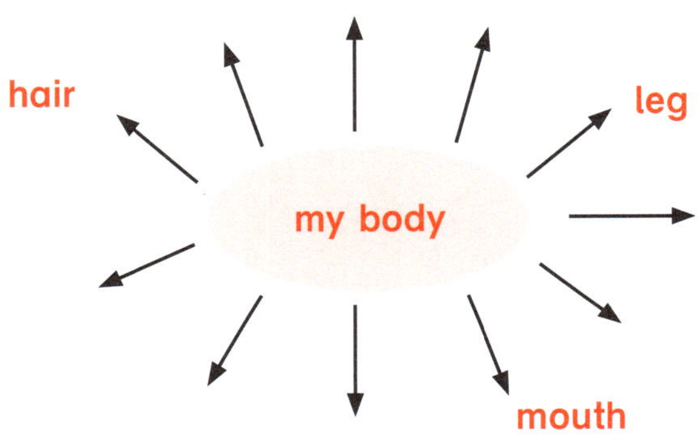

11

2 **Listen to "This is me!" and read out loud.**
Höre „This is me!“ an und sprich laut mit.

This is me!
Hi, my name is Ron.
I'm ten years old.
I have blond hair.
My telephone number is 55 43 21.
My favourite colour is blue.
I live in London.

3 **Fill in the gaps.– Vervollständige die Sätze.**

nine years • name • 12314 •
hair • pink • Berlin

Hello, my .... is Kim.

I'm .... old. I have black ....

My telephone number is ....

My favourite colour is ....

I live in ....

4 **What's this in English? Fill in the gaps.**
Kannst du das auf Englisch sagen?
Vervollständige die Sätze.

a) Sage, wie du heißt.

My .... is ....

b) Sage, wo du wohnst.

I live ....

c) Nenne deine Telefonnummer.

My ....

is ....

d) Sage, wie alt du bist.

I'm .... years ....

e) Nenne deine Haarfarbe.

I .... hair.

f) Nenne deine Lieblingsfarbe.

My.. is ....

g) Sage, dass du gerne Pizza magst.

I.. pizza.

5 **What's the answer?**
Beantworte die Fragen jetzt ohne Hilfe.

1. What's your name?
2. Where are you from?
3. How old are you?
4. What's your hobby?
5. Who's your best friend?
6. What's your favourite colour?
7. Have you got sisters or brothers?

1. ....
2. ....
3. ....
4. ....
5. ....
6. ....
7. ....

Heads, arms, shoulders ...

REGEL

Pluralformen bilden

Die **Mehrzahl (Plural)** wird meist durch das Anhängen der Endung **-s** gebildet: *one leg – two legs*.

Es gibt aber auch Ausnahmen. Endet das englische Wort mit einem **-y** (*body*) wird in der Mehrzahl aus dem *-ys* ein *-ies* (*bodies*):
one body – two bodies; baby – babies; family – families.

Es gibt noch weitere Besonderheiten: Bei einer Reihe von **Mehrzahlformen** verändert sich das **ganze** Wort. Diese muss man auswendig lernen.

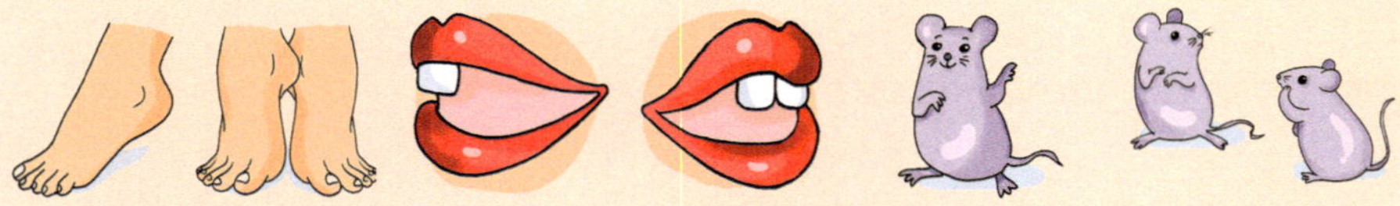

one foot two feet, one tooth two teeth, one mouse two mice

6 Fill in the gaps. – Vervollständige die Sätze.

one • three • hair • one • no •
green • three • one • eyes • legs

My monster is …………………… .

My monster has got …………… head, …………… arms, …………… shoulders, …………… nose, five …………… , …………… mouth, …………… ear, black …………… and four …………… .

7 Now draw your own monster and describe it. You can use the following words.

Male jetzt dein eigenes Monster und beschreibe es. Du kannst die folgenden Wörter verwenden.

head • arm • eye • mouth • ear • hair • leg • finger • toe • nose

TIPP
Aufgabe 6 kann dir dabei helfen.

8 Listen and fill in the right numbers.

Höre genau zu und trage die richtigen Zahlen ein.

12

TIPP
Anfangs hörst du die Körperteile der Reihe nach, später, ab „Anne“ dann durcheinander. Manche Körperteile werden vielleicht ausgelassen.

My monster has got …

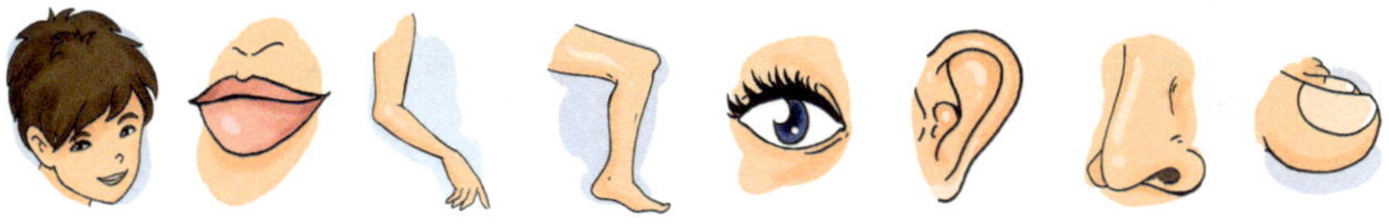

Betty								
Peter								
John								
Anne								
Mary								
Bob								
Marc								

Feelings

TIPP

Wenn man fragen möchte, wie es jemandem geht, fragt man:
How are you?
Als Antwort sagen wir auf Deutsch: Mir geht es gut.
Aber auf Englisch sagt man: *I* ***am*** *fine.*

happy

fine

sad

tired

thirsty

hungry

9 **How are you?**
Read the dialogue out aloud.
Wie geht es dir? Lies laut.

TIPP

Vielleicht findest du einen Partner für den kleinen Dialog?

10 **Write a dialogue. Fill in the bubbles. Look at the pictures in the bubbles.**
Schreibe selbst einen Dialog in die Sprechblasen.
Achte auf die Bilder in den Sprechblasen.

TIPP
Aufgabe 9 kann dir dabei helfen.

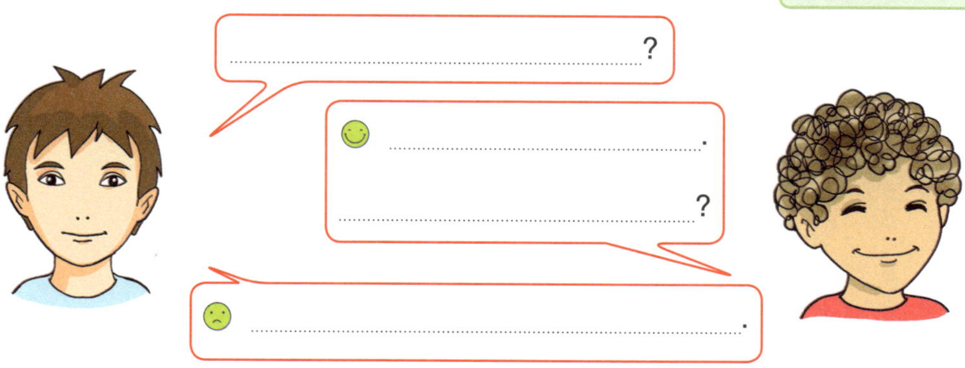

11 **Listen to the recording. – Höre gut zu.**

13

a) Connect the children's names and their pictures.
Verbinde die Namen der Kinder mit ihren Bildern.

John Bob Betty Mary Peter Anne

b) Listen again and write the sentences you hear.
Höre noch einmal die Aufnahme an und schreibe die Sätze auf, die du hörst.

13

John is ...

Zwischentest

Tick the correct answer. – Kreuze die richtige Antwort an.

1 Body

a)

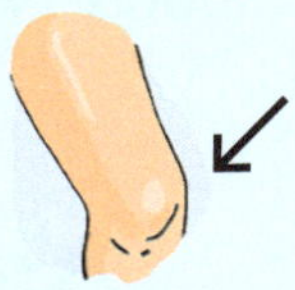

- ☐ leg
- ☐ knee
- ☐ head

b)

- ☐ ear
- ☐ eight
- ☐ eye

c)

- ☐ tou
- ☐ too
- ☐ toe

d)

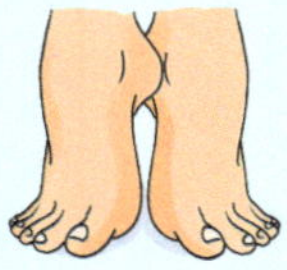

- ☐ foot
- ☐ feet
- ☐ body

e)

- ☐ nose
- ☐ hand
- ☐ hair

f)

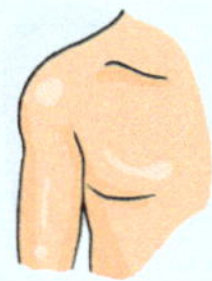

- ☐ fingers
- ☐ shoulder
- ☐ hand

maximale Punktzahl 6

2 Feelings

a)

- ☐ sad
- ☐ happy
- ☐ hungry

b)

- ☐ happy
- ☐ hungry
- ☐ thirsty

c)

- ☐ tired
- ☐ fine
- ☐ thirsty

d)

- ☐ fine
- ☐ sad
- ☐ thirsty

maximale Punktzahl 4

Gesamtpunktzahl .... von 10

Lernplaner

Kontrolliere deine Ergebnisse mithilfe der Lösungen (Seite 104) und addiere die erreichten Punkte.

☐ 10 bis 8 Punkte: ☐ 7 bis 5 Punkte: ☐ 4 bis 0 Punkte:

My family

Das lernst du hier:

- Über dich, deine Familie, deine Freunde und deine Haustiere zu sprechen und zu schreiben.
- Wie ist das mit „mein“ und „dein“ auf Englisch?

Mary's family tree
(Marys Stammbaum)

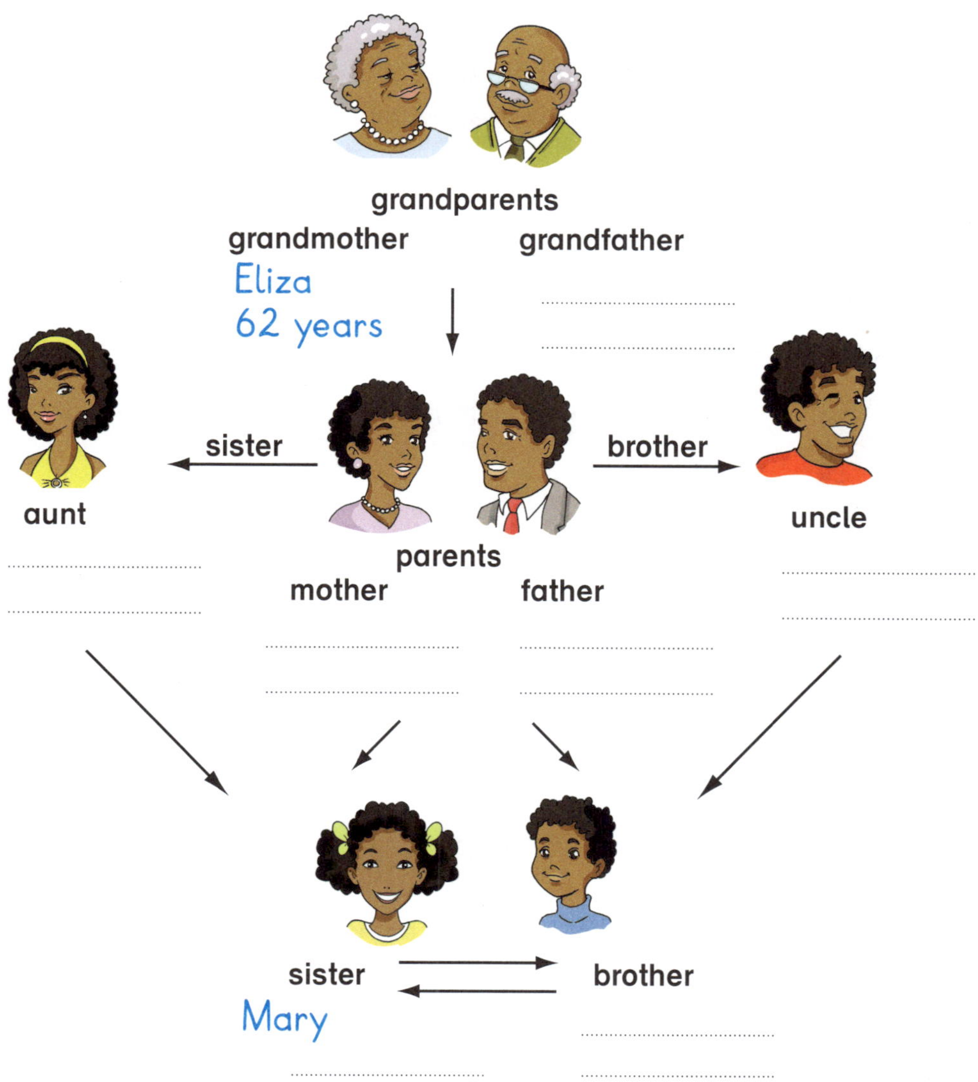

1 Mary's family

a) Read the text. – Lies den Text.

Look! This is my family. My grandmother is sixty-two years old and her name is Eliza. My grandfather's name is Paul. He is from Germany. He is sixty-five years old. My grandparents have got a house in Oxford. My mother and my father are thirty years old. My mother's name is Meggie and my father's name is Dan. My father has got a brother. His name is Steve and he is twenty-five years old. Steve is my and Simon's uncle, he is very funny. My aunt Sharon is very funny, too. She is thirty-one years old and my mother's sister. And who is Simon? Simon is my little brother. He is five years old and I am his big sister, I am ten years old.

b) Can you fill the names and the ages into the family tree now?
Kannst du die Namen und das Alter jetzt in den Stammbaum eintragen?

2 Look at the family tree again and fill in the gaps. Schau dir den Stammbaum noch einmal genau an und vervollständige die Sätze.

Sharon is my mother's .... and my .... She is .... years old.

Steve is my and my brother's .... and he is very funny.

These are my .... Eliza is my .... and Paul is my ....

My .... are Meggie and Dan.

And this little boy is my ....

He is .... years old and his name

is ....

He has got a cat family.

3 Family words

a) In jeder Zeile ist ein englisches Wort versteckt. Die übrigen Buchstaben der Zeile ergeben ein deutsches Wort.
Kreise die Buchstaben des deutschen Wortes ein. In der Zeile darunter findest du das gleiche Wort dann auf Englisch. Streiche die Buchstaben des englischen Wortes durch, es bleibt wieder ein deutsches Wort übrig … Und weiter geht es in die nächste Zeile.
There is an English word in each line. The remaining letters make a German word. Circle the letters of the German word, then find the Englisch word in the next line and cross the letters out …

G R S O S I S S M U T T T E E R R
G E L R A T N D E M R O T N H E R
P O N A K R E L E N T S
U V N A T C E R L E
F B A T H R U E D R E R
G R B O S R S O T E L H E T R E R N
G R M U A N D T T P E A R E R N T S
M G R O T O S H E S V R A T E R
G T R A A N D N T F A T E H E R
S A C H U N W E S T T E R

b) Write every German word in your exercise book and next to it the English word with the same meaning.
Schreibe alle deutschen Worte in dein Heft und direkt daneben jeweils auch das englisch Wort mit der gleichen Bedeutung.

Großmutter – grandmother ....

14

4 **This is the family of Simon's cat. Listen: Who is who?**
Dies ist Simons Katzenfamilie. Höre gut zu. Wer ist wer?

grandmother • grandfather • mother • father • kitten

a)  b)  c)  d)  e) 

a) grandmother ...... Mia ......

b) ....

c) ....

d) ....

e) ....

5 **Dog family**

a) Can you colour the dog family and draw one piece of clothing for each of them?
Kannst du die Hundefamilie bunt anmalen und für jeden Hund ein Kleidungsstück dazumalen?

This is Max,
the father.
He is yellow.
He has got blue shoes.

This is Annie,
the ....
She is ....
She has got ....

This is Mini,
Maxi's ....
......
......

This is Maxi,
Mini's ....
......
......

b) Can you draw the grandparents? Write sentences about them, too.
Kannst du die Großeltern malen? Schreibe passende Sätze.

	grandmother	This is ....
	grandfather	This is ....

6 **Find the pairs and write them into the snake.**
Finde jeweils das passende Wort und schreibe es in die Schlange.

old • you • big • mother • aunt • she •
boy • old • ~~sister~~ • grandfather

Identity cards

7 Read the cards. Write your own cards and fill in the gaps.
Lies die Karten. Schreibe deine eigenen Karten und fülle sie vollständig aus.

Name: Mary
Age: 10
Telephone number: 0432 – 236750

This is me!
My name is Mary.
I'm 10 years old.
My telephone number is 0432–236750.

This is me!

.... name

is ....

.... years old.

.... telephone number

is ....

Name:
Age:
Telephone number:

Name: Anne
Age: 11
Telephone number: 0432 – 569034

This is my friend!
Her name is Anne.
She is 11 years old.
Her telephone number is 0432–569034.

This is my friend!

Her name

is ....

.... years old.

.... telephone number

is ....

Name:
Age:
Telephone number:

Name: Peter
Age: 11
Telephone number: 0431–231134

This is my friend!
His name is Peter.
He is 11 years old.
His telephone number is 0431–231134.

Name:
Age:
Telephone number:

This is my friend!

His name

is ....

.... years old.

.... telephone number

is ....

REGEL

Possessivpronomen (besitzanzeigendes Fürwort)

I ↔ ***my***	***he*** ↔ ***his***	***she*** ↔ ***her***
I *am Mary.*	***He*** *has got a dog.*	***She*** *is thirteen.*
My *name is Mary.*	***His*** *dog is young.*	***Her*** *birthday is in April.*

A teacher is asking Mary.

What's **your** name?

My name is Mary.

How old are **you**?

I'm 10 years old.

Mary, when is **your** birthday?

My birthday is in August.

REGEL

Possessivpronomen (besitzanzeigendes Fürwort)

you* ↔ *your	***they* ↔ *their***
*Have **you** got a brother?*	***They** have got a cat.*
*Is **your** brother nice?*	***Their** cat is black and white.*

15

8 Mary's friends

a) Listen and complete the chart.
Höre gut zu und vervollständige die Tabelle.

Name:	Anne		
Age:	11 years		
Birthday:	in August		

b) Can you write sentences about the boys?
Kannst du Sätze über die Jungen schreiben?

Beispiel: *Anne is Mary's friend. She is eleven years old. Her birthday is in August.*

REGEL

Possessivpronomen (besitzanzeigendes Fürwort)

we* ↔ *our	***you* ↔ *your***
***We** have got a car.*	***You** are nice children.*
***Our** car is old.*	***Your** parents are lucky.*

Friends are talking

9 **Read the sentences. Then find the matching picture, colour it and write down the right letter.**
Lies die Sätze. Finde das passende Bild, male es an und schreibe den richtigen Buchstaben in das Kästchen.

B

L

T

O

A

I

K

Y

C

S

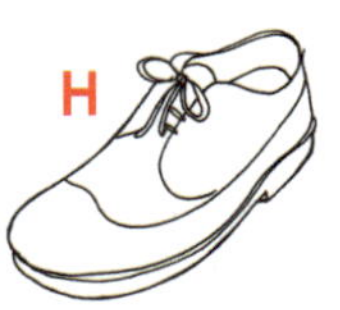
H

1. **I** have got a nice cat. Look, **my** cat is black and white. Picture: B
2. Have **you** got a new t-shirt? **Your** new blue t-shirt is great. Picture:
3. **He** is a nice grandfather. Look, **his** hair is grey. Picture:
4. Has **she** got a yellow teddy bear? No, **she** hasn't. **Her** teddy bear is brown. Picture:
5. **It** is a big shoe. **Its** colour is yellow. Picture:
6. **We** have got a red car. **Our** car is very old. Picture:
7. Mary and Simon, **you** have got a nice uncle. **Your** uncle is very funny with his pink coat. Picture:
8. Have **they** got brown eyes? No, **they** haven't. **Their** eyes are blue. Picture:

D

R

M

E

M

Where are the friends? Write down the letters from 1. to 8. into the boxes.
Wo sind die Freunde? Schreibe die Buchstaben von 1. bis 8. in die Kästchen.

The friends are at a B 1 _ 2 _ 3 _ 4 _ 5 _ 6 _ 7 _ 8 party.

REGEL

Übersicht der Possessivpronomen

Subjektform	Possessivpronomen
I – ich	*my* – mein(e)
you – du	*your* – dein(e)
he – er	*his* – sein(e)
she – sie	*her* – ihr(e)
it – es	*its* – sein(e)/ihr(e)
we – wir	*our* – unser(e)
you – ihr	*your* – euer(e)
they – sie	*their* – ihr(e)

The pronoun sun

10 **For experts. Can you complete the sun?**
Für Experten. Kannst du die Sonne vervollständigen?
your • she • its • our • you • he • they

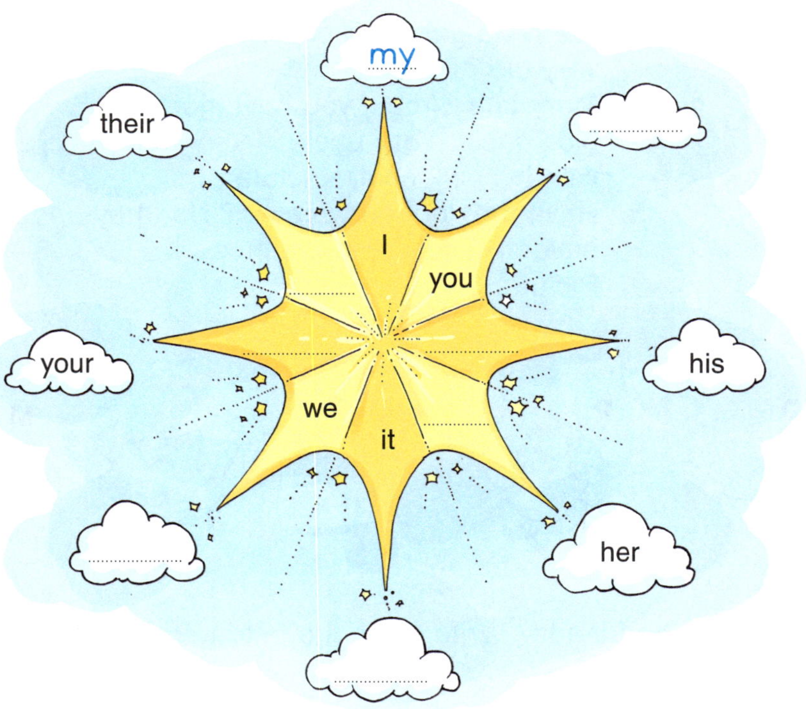

11 **Translate only the underlined parts of the sentences into English.**
Übersetze nur die unterstrichenen Teile der Sätze ins Englische.

a) Bob bekommt ein Skateboard zu (= for) seinem Geburtstag.

b) Meine Schwester schenkt ihm eine CD.

c) Die kleine Maus rennt in ihr Haus.

d) Anne räumt ihr Zimmer jeden Abend auf.

e) John hat deinen Fußball in seinem Schrank versteckt.

f) Die Kinder legen ihre Jacken neben ihre Schultaschen.

g) Die Lehrerin gibt uns unsere Hefte zurück.

h) Euer neues Auto ist wirklich schön, seine Farbe gefällt mir gut.

i) Meine Mutter hilft mir immer mit meinen Hausaufgaben.

Zwischentest

1 Tick the right answer.
Kreuze die richtige Antwort an.

a) My father and my mother are my
- ☐ grandparents.
- ☐ parents.
- ☐ aunts.

b) My father's brother is my
- ☐ aunt.
- ☐ brother.
- ☐ uncle.

c) My father's father is my
- ☐ grandfather.
- ☐ uncle.
- ☐ grandparents.

d) Tom's father's father is
- ☐ my grandfather.
- ☐ his grandfather.
- ☐ her grandparents.

e) Mary's father's brother is
- ☐ her father.
- ☐ my uncle.
- ☐ her uncle.

f) What's your name?
- ☐ Her name is … .
- ☐ My name is … .
- ☐ Your name is … .

g) How old are they?
- ☐ He is 5 years old.
- ☐ They are 10 years old.
- ☐ I am 10 years old.

h) How old is Julian?
- ☐ 11 years is he old.
- ☐ He is 11 years old.
- ☐ His birthday is in September.

i) When is Lisa's birthday?
- ☐ His birthday is in August.
- ☐ She is birthday is in August.
- ☐ Her birthday is in August.

j) What's Mary's and Simon's telephone number?
- ☐ Their telephone number is 0432-236750.
- ☐ Our telephone number is 0432-236750.
- ☐ They are telephone number 0432-236750.

Gesamtpunktzahl

.... von 10

Lernplaner

Kontrolliere deine Ergebnisse mithilfe der Lösungen (Seite 105) und addiere die erreichten Punkte.

☐ 10 bis 8 Punkte: ☐ 7 bis 5 Punkte: ☐ 4 bis 0 Punkte:

At home

Das lernst du hier:

- Dein Zimmer, eure Wohnung, euer Haus zu beschreiben.
- Auch *in, on, under* oder *next to* wird dir keine Schwierigkeiten mehr bereiten.

Bob's home

1 Look at the pictures and listen to the recording.
Can you match the words with the objects?
Sieh dir die Bilder an und höre gut zu.
Kannst du die Wörter mit den Objekten verbinden?

16

garden car three windows garage door

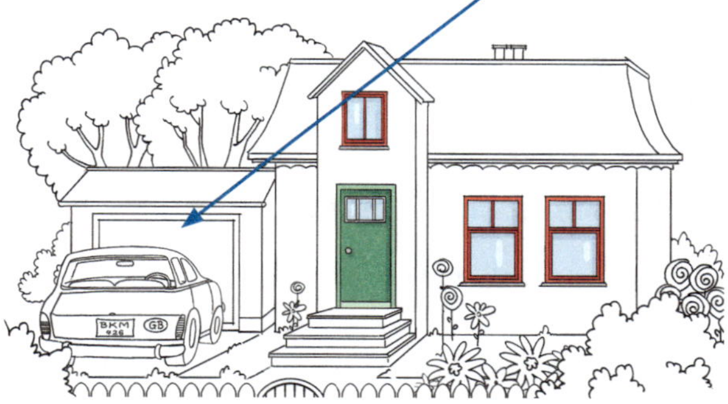

wardrobe two posters wall two windows

teddy bear bed carpet floor

door computer desk chair

2 Jumbled words – Schüttelwörter

Bob's family has got a .... (osueh) with a .... (aredng). There is a .... (agraeg) for the .... (rca).

The house has got three .... (wdosniw) and a green .... (ordo).

In Bob's .... (orom) is a .... (sekd) and a .... (archi). The teddy bear is on the .... (edb).

And there is a .... (rdroebaw) for the clothes. The blue .... (petrac) is on the .... (olfor).

And there are two posters on the .... (alwl), too.

3 Now, listen to the recording again and find 14 mistakes in the text. Correct them.

Höre die Aufnahme noch einmal an und finde die 14 Fehler im Text. Korrigiere sie.

17

This is Bob's ~~house~~ home. His family has got a house with a chair and a table for the car. The garden has got three red windows and a green window. This is Bob's room. The house has got two big doors and under the right window is a carpet with a chair. On the desk is a book. In the room is a bed, too. There is a teddy bear on the desk. Next to the bed is a chair for the clothes. It is green. And there is a blue poster in the middle of the room on the wall. The door is to the right. Next to the door are two books on the floor. Bob is a big fan of Garfield!

In a room

4 **Find the right preposition and write sentences.**
Ordne jedem Bild die richtige Präposition zu und schreibe einen Satz.

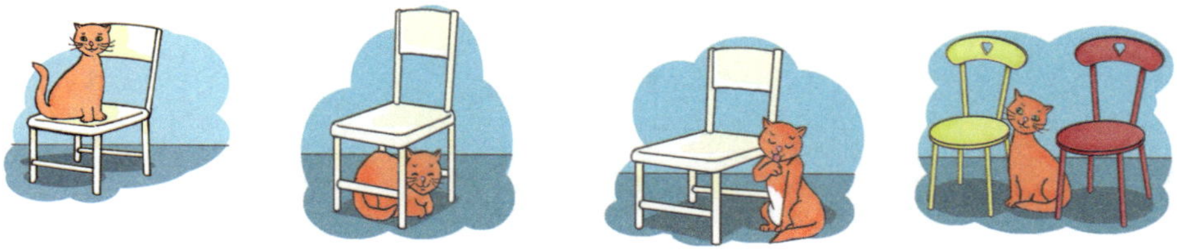

The cat is on the chair. ....

....

REGEL

Prepositions of place – **Präpositionen** (Verhältniswort) **des Ortes**

inside, in – in	*next to* – neben	*under* – unter
on – auf	*in front of* – vor	*between* – zwischen

5 **Look at the picture and fill the gaps with the right preposition.**
Sieh dir das Bild an und setze jeweils die richtige Präposition ein.

The poster is on the wall. There is a wardrobe .... the room. The teddy bear is .... the chair. The window is .... the door. The clothes are .... the door. The carpet is .... the floor. A coat is .... the wardrobe. The bed is .... the window. The cap is .... the coat. The cars are .... the bed.

6 **Colour all the fields with "house words" red.**
Male alle Felder mit Wörtern, die mit „Haus" zu tun haben, rot an.

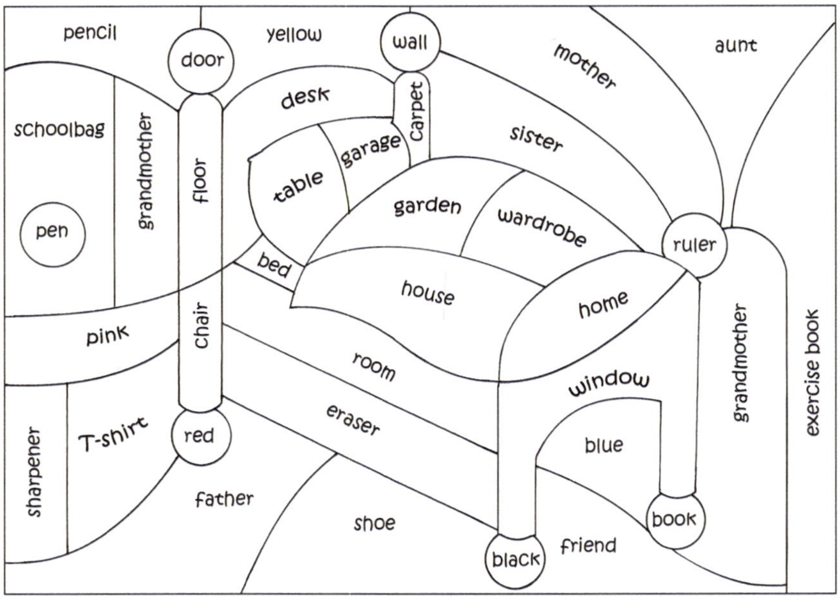

The .... is red.

7 **The children's rooms**

a) Look at the pictures and tick the right answer.
Sieh dir die Bilder an und kreuze die richtige Antwort an.

The bed is
- ☐ under the poster.
- ☐ next to the poster.
- ☐ on the poster.

The sweatshirt is
- ☐ on the wardrobe.
- ☐ in the wardrobe.
- ☐ next to the wardrobe.

Picture 1: ....

The car is
- ☐ under the bed.
- ☐ on the bed.
- ☐ in the bed.

The wardrobe is
- ☐ on the bed.
- ☐ under the poster.
- ☐ next to the bed.

Picture 2: ....

The poster is
- ☐ on the bed.
- ☐ on the wall.
- ☐ next to the wall.

The teddy bear is
- ☐ on the wardrobe.
- ☐ under the wardrobe.
- ☐ in the wardrobe.

Picture 3: ....

b) Look at the pictures again and listen to the recording.
Is it Anne's, Peter's or John's room?
Write the names on the line under the pictures.
Sieh dir die Bilder noch einmal an und höre dir die Aufnahme an.
Ist es Annes, Peters oder Johns Zimmer?
Schreibe die Namen auf die Linie unter den Bildern.

18

8 Your room

a) Describe your room. The words in the box can help you.
Beschreibe dein Zimmer. Was gibt es dort/dort nicht?
Die Wörter im Kasten helfen dir dabei.

Poster Schrank Schreibtisch Teppich Katze Bett Hund
Teddybär Bücher Stuhl Fenster Computer

Example: *I have got a CD player in my room.*
I haven't got a TV in my room.

b) Now answer the questions.
Beantworte jetzt die Fragen.
Use: Yes, I have./No, I haven't.

Have you got a desk in your room? ....

Have you got a computer in your room? ....

Have you got a football in your room? ....

Have you got a skateboard in your room? ....

Have you got animal posters in your room? ....

9 Crossword
Kreuzworträtsel

a) Can you find 12 "house words"? Circle them.
Findest du 12 Wörter, die mit „Haus" zu tun haben? Kreise sie ein.

b) Write them down.
Schreibe sie auf.

D	E	S	B	W	C	H	A	I	R
O	O	F	G	I	G	C	A	A	H
O	W	O	A	N	A	P	R	D	D
N	W	A	R	D	R	O	B	E	E
H	A	F	D	O	A	S	R	L	S
O	L	L	E	W	G	O	O	P	K
U	L	O	N	B	E	D	O	N	M
S	D	O	O	E	S	S	M	D	K
E	N	R	B	C	A	R	P	E	T

10 Look at the picture for a minute.
Then cover the page and tick the correct box.
Sieh dir das Bild eine Minute lang an.
Decke dann die Seite ab und kreuze die passenden Kästchen an.

In Mary's room there is/are

☐ an eraser	☐ a pair of scissors	☐ a schoolbag
☐ a coat	☐ dresses	☐ a ruler
☐ a garage	☐ a garden	☐ a book
☐ a wardrobe	☐ a window	☐ a carpet
☐ a ball	☐ a teddy bear	☐ a pencil case
☐ one car	☐ two cars	☐ three cars
☐ one shoe	☐ two shoes	☐ three shoes
☐ one poster	☐ two posters	☐ three posters

11 Look at the picture again.
Match the sentences and write them down.
Sieh dir das Bild noch einmal an.
Verbinde die passenden Wörter und schreibe die Sätze ins Heft.

The teddy bear	is	on	the bed.
Two shoes		in	the wall.
The dresses		under	the wardrobe.
The schoolbag	are	next to	the desk.
A book			the chair.
The bed			the wardrobe.
The poster			the box.
The car			the desk.
The ball			the wardrobe.

12 Peter's house
a) Read the text.
Lies dir den Text genau durch.

Peter's house is in Oxford Street. It has got a big garage for two cars but only a small garden behind the house. In the garden is a tree. The garage is next to the hall. There are two bedrooms. The living room is very big. It has got three windows and one door. The kitchen is next to the living room. The bathroom is small. There is no window.

b) Is this Peter's house? Explain why or why not.
Ist das Peters Haus? Erkläre warum/warum nicht.
Start like this: This is/This is not Peter's house, because it has ...

13 My dream house

a) Draw a picture of your dream house and colour the rooms.
Male ein Bild von deinem Traumhaus und male die Zimmer bunt an.

b) Then write 5 sentences about it. Use the words from the box.
Beschreibe dein Haus dann in 5 Sätzen. Benutze dabei die Wörter aus dem Kasten.

under, yellow, blue, window, car, garage, in, living room, kitchen, green, bathroom, room, on, door, next to, garden, bedroom

Example: *My dream house has got five rooms, a garage and a garden. The garage is red. The living room is yellow. It is over the kitchen, the bedroom is under the bathroom ...*

Zwischentest

1 Tick the right answer. – Kreuze die richtige Antwort an.

a) 

This is
- ☐ a floor.
- ☐ a window.
- ☐ a door.

b) 

This is
- ☐ a wardrobe.
- ☐ a carpet.
- ☐ a desk.

maximale Punktzahl 2

2 Odd one out. – Was passt nicht?

a) ☐ wall ☐ car ☐ floor

b) ☐ window ☐ door ☐ poster

c) ☐ in ☐ chair ☐ on

d) ☐ under ☐ next to ☐ and

maximale Punktzahl 4

3 Tick the right answer. – Kreuze die richtige Antwort an.

a) 

The cat is
- ☐ on the table.
- ☐ under the table.
- ☐ next to the table.

b) 

The cat is
- ☐ under Tim.
- ☐ on Tim.
- ☐ next to Tim.

c) 

The poster is
- ☐ on the floor next to the chair.
- ☐ on the wall next to the chair.
- ☐ on the wall next to the desk.

d) 

The bed is
- ☐ on the floor next to the window.
- ☐ in the floor next to the window.
- ☐ on the floor under the window.

maximale Punktzahl 4

Kontrolliere deine Ergebnisse mithilfe der Lösungen (Seite 106) und addiere die erreichten Punkte.

☐ 10 bis 8 Punkte: ☐ 7 bis 5 Punkte: ☐ 4 bis 0 Punkte:

Lernplaner

Gesamtpunktzahl .... von 10

Food and time

Das lernst du hier:

- ➞ Wie du sagen kannst, was du gerne isst – und wie du jemanden danach fragst.
- ➞ Wie du Auskunft über die Zeit gibst und wie du danach fragst.

Breakfast

1 Copy the words. – Schreibe die Wörter noch einmal richtig ab.

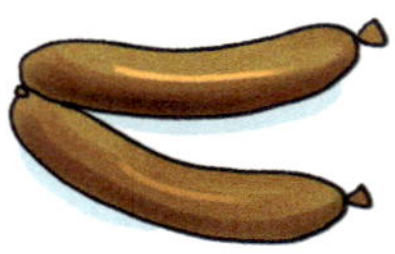
sausages

butter

cheese

toast

orange juice

tea

jam

eggs

cereal

cornflakes

milk

TIPP

Ein englisches Frühstück ist anders, als wir es gewohnt sind. Meist gibt es nicht nur Toast mit Konfitüre/Marmelade, sondern davor bereits *cornflakes*, *muesli*, *porridge* (Haferschleim) oder eine andere Art von *cereal* (Frühstücksflocken). Dazu schmeckt den Engländern eine Tasse Tee mit Milch. Das *full English breakfast*, das es nicht jeden Tag gibt, besteht aus Toast, *baked beans* (gebackene Bohnen), *bacon and eggs* (Speck mit Ei), gebratenen Champignons oder/und Tomaten.

2 **To have breakfast – Frühstücken**
Connect the objects to the words.
Verbinde die Objekte mit den Wörtern.

eggs milk tea orange juice

cornflakes butter

jam sausages

toast cheese

TIPP

Die Engländer essen gerne **marmalade**, sie wird aus Zitrusfrüchten gemacht.
„Unsere" Marmelade (Erdbeere, Kirsche, …) heißt auf Englisch **jam**.
strawberry jam = Erdbeermarmelade (oder wie es offiziell richtig heißt: Erdbeerkonfitüre)

Fruit

3 **What can you see in the picture?**
Was siehst du auf dem Bild?

Start like this:
I can see two apples …

4 **What do you (not) like?**
Was magst du (nicht so) gerne?

I like oranges.

I don't like melons.

TIPP

Wenn man sagen möchte, dass man eine Frucht mag, muss die Frucht in der Mehrzahl stehen. Auf Deutsch sage ich auch: „Ich mag Orangen."

I like strawberries.

I don't like strawberries.

a)  or ……………………

b)  or ……………………

c)  or ……………………

d)  or ……………………

e)  or ……………………

f)  or ……………………

TIPP

In Großbritannien kaufen die meisten Menschen Obst und Gemüse in sehr großen Supermärkten ein. Diese *supermarkets* haben häufig bis spät in die Nacht und sogar am Sonntag geöffnet. Auch die Bestellung im Internet mit Lieferung am nächsten Tag ist bei vielen Supermarktketten möglich.

Lunch and dinner

5 **Connect the pictures and the words.**
Verbinde jedes Bild mit dem passenden Wort.

> TIPP
> *breakfast* – Frühstück
> *lunch* – Mittagessen
> *dinner* – Abendessen

chips

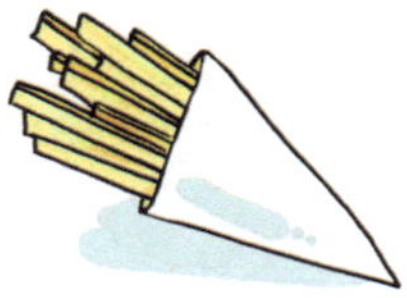

sandwich

spaghetti

hamburger

hot dog

fish and chips

fish

pizza

6 **Plural forms**
Do you know the plural form of the following words?
Wie lautet der Plural (= die Mehrzahl) dieser Wörter?

a) apple .... b) cherry ....

c) lemon .... d) drink ....

e) strawberry .... f) orange ....

g) sandwich .... h) fish ....

i) pizza .... j) melon ....

7 Write the words. Mind your spelling!
Schreibe die Wörter auf die Zeilen.
Achte dabei auf die Rechtschreibung.

o o h g t d

....

a e i p t g t h s

....

w h s i d n a c

....

h a i f p s s i h n c d

....

r r e a m g h b u

....

z p i a z

....

8 Connect the words.
Verbinde die Wörter.

hot dog		fish
orange juice	breakfast	chips
tea		strawberry
spaghetti		hamburger
banana	lunch dinner	pizza
pineapple		cereal

TIPP

Manche Wörter passen bei *breakfast* und bei *lunch/dinner*.

9 What do the children like? Listen and tick the right answer.
Was essen die Kinder gerne?
Höre gut zu und kreuze die richtige Antwort an.

19

Betty

Mary

Anne

Peter

John

Bob

10 Underline the odd word.
Welches Wort passt nicht? Unterstreiche es.

Beispiel: *brother · sister · monster · father*

a) apple · banana · spaghetti · cherry

b) milk · orange juice · tea · cheese

c) knife · cup · fork · spoon

d) hamburger · hot dog · banana · chips

e) cornflakes · milk · pizza · toast

Time

REGEL

Nur beim Nennen der vollen Stunden verwendet man o'clock.

Achtung:

Wie spät ist es? = ***What's** the time?*

11 **Draw the hands.**

Zeichne die Zeiger der Uhr richtig ein.

It's nine o'clock.

It's eight o'clock.

It's three o'clock.

It's twelve o'clock.

TIPP

Man kann die Uhrzeit auch mit dem Zusatz *am/pm* ausdrücken.

am (= vormittags) steht für alle Zeiten von
Mitternacht bis 12 Uhr mittags.
It's 8 am = Es ist acht Uhr morgens.

pm (= nachmittags) steht für alle Zeiten von
12 Uhr mittags bis Mitternacht.
It's 8 pm = Es ist acht Uhr abends.
Man kann *o'clock* und *am/pm* **nicht gleichzeitig** benutzen!

12 **What's the time? Draw the missing hands and write down the time.**
Wie spät ist es? Zeichne die fehlenden Zeiger ein und schreibe die Uhrzeit auf.

It's two o'clock.

a)

It's ten o'clock.

b)

It's eleven o'clock.

c)

It's five o'clock.

d)

It's ....

....

e)

....

....

f)

....

....

g)

....

....

TIPP

Achtung: Die Armbanduhr heißt auf Englisch *watch*. Aber die Frage: „Wie viel Uhr ist es?" lautet *What's the time?* oder *What time is it?*

13 **Peter asks Betty: “Do you like … for … ?”**
Peter fragt Betty: „Magst du … zum …?“

Do you like pizza for breakfast, Betty?

No, I don’t like pizza for breakfast.

(tea / breakfast)
Do you like tea for breakfast, Betty?

Yes, I like tea for breakfast.

(cereal / milk / breakfast)
Do you like ……………………………………………………

Yes, ……………………………………………………
……………………………………………………

(toast / jam / dinner)
Do ……………………………………………………

……………………………………………………
……………………………………………………

(fish and chips/lunch)

14 Breakfast at Betty's house.

Look at the pictures and write.

Schaue dir die Bilder an und schreibe den Text.

It's  at Betty's  .  and Peter are hungry.

Everything is on the  for breakfast. There are  ,  , 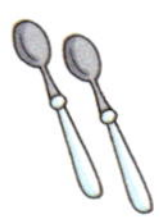 , plates, cups and glasses. There is  and there is 

. Betty likes  and cornflakes. Peter likes  and  with  .

Zwischentest

1 Food

a) 

- ☐ pineapple
- ☐ banana
- ☐ pear

b) 

- ☐ melons
- ☐ cherries
- ☐ oranges

c) 

- ☐ melon
- ☐ strawberrry
- ☐ lemon

d) 

- ☐ cereal
- ☐ hot dog
- ☐ cheese

e) 

- ☐ pommes
- ☐ sausage
- ☐ chips

f) 

- ☐ the
- ☐ tea
- ☐ tee

maximale Punktzahl 6

2 Time

a) 

- ☐ four o'clock
- ☐ five o'clock
- ☐ six o'clock

b) 

- ☐ eleven o'clock
- ☐ two o'clock
- ☐ three o'clock

c) 

- ☐ seven o'clock
- ☐ nine o'clock
- ☐ ten o'clock

d) 

- ☐ eight o'clock
- ☐ four o'clock
- ☐ three o'clock

maximale Punktzahl 4

Gesamtpunktzahl

.... von 10

Kontrolliere deine Ergebnisse mithilfe der Lösungen (Seite 108) und addiere die erreichten Punkte.

☐ 10 bis 8 Punkte: ☐ 7 bis 5 Punkte: ☐ 4 bis 0 Punkte:

Nature

Das lernst du hier:

- → Wie die Tiere auf einem Bauernhof bezeichnet werden.
- → Wie du Sätze in Einzahl (Singular) und Mehrzahl (Plural) bildest.
- → Welche Tiere du im Zoo siehst.
- → Wie die Haustiere heißen.
- → Wie du das Wetter beschreibst.

Farm animals

1 Connect the words and the pictures.
Which words are new for you?
Verbinde die Wörter mit den Bildern.
Welche Wörter sind neu für dich?

REGEL

Einzahl (Singular) *This is a cat.*

Wenn du von einem Tier/Gegenstand nur eines sehen kannst, sagst du beispielsweise: *“This is a cat.”* (Dies ist eine Katze.)

Mehrzahl (Plural) *These are three cats.*

Wenn du zwei oder noch mehr Tiere/Gegenstände sehen kannst, sagst du beispielsweise *“These are cats.”* (Dies sind Katzen.)
Achtung: Hier musst du an das **Hauptwort/Substantiv** ein **-s** anhängen:
Wenn du die **Anzahl** dazuschreibst, heißt es:
*“These are three cat**s**.”* (Dies sind drei Katzen.)

2 **Now it’s your turn. Make sentences.**
Jetzt bist du dran. Bilde Sätze.

a)

Beispiel: *This is a pig.*

b) 

These are four horses. These are ...

c) Listen and correct your sentences.
Höre gut zu und korrigiere deine Sätze.

20

REGEL

Bei den meisten Nomen (Hauptwörtern) wird der Plural (die Mehrzahl) durch das einfache Anhängen von **-s** gebildet. Endet die Singularform (die Einzahl) mit einem Zischlaut, hängt man **-es** an (z. B.: *buses, boxes*).

Aufgepasst, unregelmäßige Formen:

baby – babies *wife – wives* *tomato – tomatoes*
family – families *knife – knives* *potato – potatoes*
man – men *woman – women* *child – children*
sheep – sheep
fish – fish (nur wenn man von mehreren Fischarten spricht: *fishes)*

Zoo animals

3 Connect the words and the pictures.
Verbinde die Wörter mit den Bildern.

monkey
elephant
giraffe
bear
zebra
hippo
lion

4 Colour the pictures of excercise 3 in the right colour.
Male die Bilder von Aufgabe 3 mit der richtigen Farbe an.

Colour the lion blue.

Colour the hippo brown.

Colour the monkey green.

Colour the zebra yellow.

Colour the elephant red.

Colour the bear orange.

Colour the giraffe grey.

Pets

5 Find seven pets. – Finde sieben Haustiere.

M	E	I	U	O	E	R	R
O	C	A	T	Y	X	P	P
U	X	Y	W	G	B	H	H
S	R	A	B	B	I	T	H
E	F	W	T	T	R	L	H
L	I	Z	B	E	D	O	G
N	S	Z	I	E	I	U	O
L	H	A	M	S	T	E	R

6 Write sentences. – Schreibe Sätze.

Beispiel: *The cat is on the chair.*

....

....

....

....

....

TIPP

Wenn etwas auf einem Bild zu sehen ist, sagt man auf Englisch immer *in (the picture). On the picture* bedeutet, dass etwas (oben) auf dem Bild drauf liegt.
I can see a dog in the picture! – Auf dem Bild kann ich einen Hund sehen!

Weather

7 Do you know 8 "weather words"?
Kennst du 8 Wörter zum Thema Wetter? Schreibe sie auf.

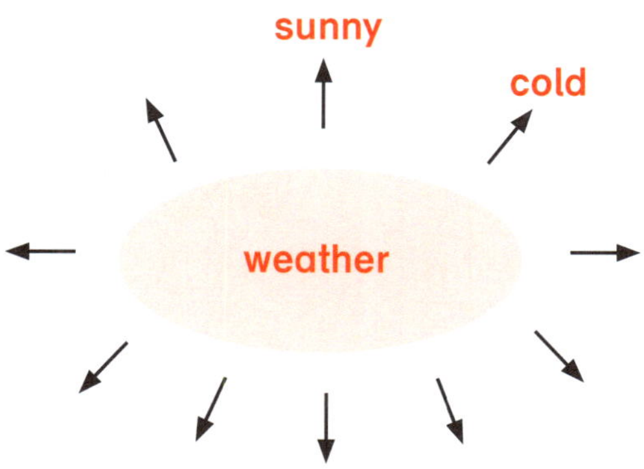

8 Scrambled letters: "weather words"
Find the correct words. – Wie heißen die Wörter richtig?

a) nusny – sunny
awmr – ....
ocld – ....
lcdous – ....
nwidy – ....
eowshr – ....

b) ayrin – ....
sown – ....
fgogy – ....
sinnushe – ....
mepraettrue – ....

9 Write the right sentence next to the picture.
Schreibe den passenden Satz jeweils neben das Bild.
It is hot. • It is cold. • It is sunny. • It is foggy. • It is windy. •
It is cloudy. • It is raining. • It is snowing.

a)  ....

b)  ....

e)  ....

f)  ....

c)  ....

g) 

....

d)  ....

h) 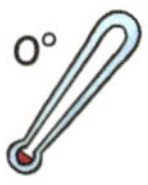

....

10 **What's the weather like in Great Britain and Ireland? Listen to the recording and draw the weather symbols. Wie ist das Wetter in Großbritannien und Irland? Höre gut zu und zeichne die Wettersymbole am richtigen Ort ein.**

21

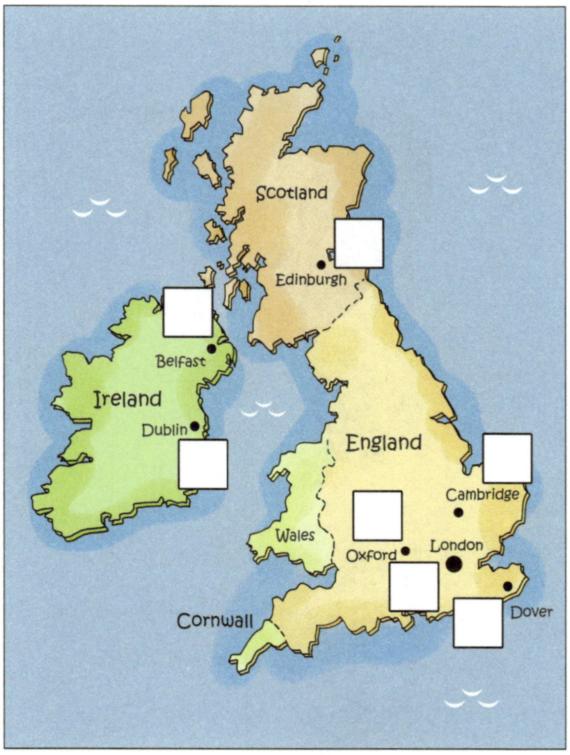

11 **My favourite weather**

a) Draw a picture of your favourite weather.
Male ein Bild von deinem Lieblingswetter.

b) Describe your favourite weather, why you like it, and what you like to do during this weather.
Beschreibe dein Lieblingswetter, sage, warum du es magst und was du bei diesem Wetter gerne machst.

My favourite weather is ...

....

....

....

Zwischentest

1 Tick the correct word. – Kreuze das richtige Wort an.

a) 

- ☐ cat
- ☐ mouse
- ☐ pig

b) 

- ☐ cow
- ☐ rooster
- ☐ sheep

c) 

- ☐ elephant
- ☐ lion
- ☐ hippo

d) 

- ☐ bear
- ☐ giraffe
- ☐ monkey

e) 

- ☐ bear
- ☐ bird
- ☐ hamster

f) 

- ☐ fish
- ☐ rooster
- ☐ rabbit

g) 

- ☐ hamster
- ☐ bird
- ☐ mouse

h) 

- ☐ rooster
- ☐ rabbit
- ☐ bear

i) 

- ☐ It's sunny.
- ☐ It's foggy.
- ☐ It's rainy.

j) 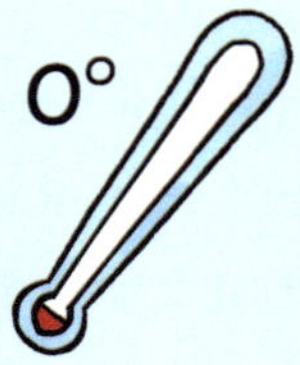

- ☐ It's foggy.
- ☐ It's hot.
- ☐ It's cold.

Gesamtpunktzahl
.... von 10

Lernplaner

Kontrolliere deine Ergebnisse mithilfe der Lösungen (Seite 109) und addiere die erreichten Punkte.

☐ 10 bis 8 Punkte: ☐ 7 bis 5 Punkte: ☐ 4 bis 0 Punkte:

My free time

Das lernst du hier:

- Freizeit macht Spaß – auch auf Englisch.
- Signalwörter, wie *just* und *still* machen das *present progressive* zu einem Kinderspiel.

Free time

1 **First learn the following words.**
You may know some of them already.
Lerne zuerst die folgenden Wörter.
Einige davon kennst du bestimmt schon.

to climb	klettern
to do	etwas machen / ausführen
to draw	zeichnen
to drink	trinken
to eat	essen
to fish	angeln
to have	etwas haben
to hear	hören
to listen to	an-/zuhören
to play	spielen
to read	*lesen*

to ride	reiten
to ride a bike	Fahrrad fahren
to see	*sehen*
to sing	singen
to swim	schwimmen
to watch	beobachten / anschauen
to write	schreiben
bike	Fahrrad
guitar	Gitarre
judo	Judo

TIPP

Achtung: *to hear* = hören — *to listen to* = anhören / zuhören
to see = sehen — *to watch* = beobachten / anschauen

Beispiel: *I can hear some noise.* — *Bob is listening to a CD.*

TIPP

Cleveres Vokabellernen

1. Schreibe die Vokabeln ab und überprüfe die Schreibweise.
2. Sage die Wörter immer laut auf (vom Deutschen in die Fremdsprache) und lerne sie in beide Richtungen: Deutsch-Englisch **und** Englisch-Deutsch.
3. Wiederhole die Vokabeln etwa 5–10 Minuten nach dem ersten Lernen. Nimm dir am Abend alle neuen Vokabeln nochmals vor.
4. Markiere alle Wörter, die dir schwerfallen. Mit diesen Wörtern kannst du beispielsweise ein Lernplakat gestalten.
6. Mache dir die Vokabeln „merkwürdig“: Nutze Bilder, merke dir Eselsbrücken, merke dir Wortpaare (Wörter gleicher oder gegensätzlicher Bedeutung), denke dir zu neuen Wörtern Geschichten aus …

Und lerne häppchenweise. 10 Vokabeln oder Redewendungen am Tag sind genug. Kümmere dich dafür aber jeden Tag um deinen Wortschatz. Vergiss nicht, immer wieder ältere Vokabeln zu wiederholen!

2 **Look at the pictures and fill in the gaps.**
Sieh dir die Bilder an und vervollständige die Sätze.

cards · tea · his name · his homework · water · a CD · a picture · the guitar · ~~a book~~ · TV · a song · a piece of toast

a)

John is reading a book.

Betty is drawing ....

Bob is writing ....

b)

Peter and Bob are playing ....

Betty and Mary are having ....

Anne and John are listening to ....

c)

John is playing

Peter is doing

Bob and John are watching

d)

Mary is eating

Betty and Anne are singing

Peter is drinking

REGEL

Wenn man ausdrücken will, dass jemand etwas gerade macht, benutzt man die **Verlaufsform** des Verbs, das ***present progressive***.
Das *present progressive* wird in der dritten Person **Singular** mit is + verb + -ing gebildet: *Bob is reading a book.*
Das *present progressive* wird in der dritten Person **Plural** mit are + verb + -ing gebildet: *Bob and John are playing basketball.*
In der deutschen Sprache gibt es diese Verlaufsform nicht.
Wenn du die Verben im *present progressive* schreibst, musst du folgende Regeln beachten:

- Bei Verben, die mit einem (stummen, also nicht gesprochenen) *-e* enden, wird bei der Bildung der *-ing*-Form der Endbuchstabe *-e* weggelassen: *write – writing.*
- Bei Verben, die mit einem kurzen Vokal (Selbstlaut) und folgendem Konsonanten (Mitlaut) (z. B.: *-m, -n, -p oder -t*) enden, wird der Konsonant verdoppelt: *swim – swimming, run – running.*

TIPP

Verb heißt auch Tunwort, Tätigkeitswort oder Zeitwort.

3 **What is wrong? Correct the mistakes.**
Was ist falsch? Korrigiere die Fehler.

Betty is ~~writing~~ a picture.

Betty is drawing a picture.

John is doing the guitar.

....

Peter is eating water.

....

Peter is watching his homework.

....

John is drawing a book.

....

Bob is reading his name.

....

Mary is singing a piece of toast.

....

Bob and John are doing TV.

....

Anne and John are playing a CD.

....

In the garden

4 Look at the picture. Then read the sentences and tick "right" or "wrong". Correct the wrong sentences.
Sieh dir das Bild an. Dann lies die Sätze und kreuze „richtig" oder „falsch" an. Korrigiere die falschen Sätze.

		right	wrong
a)	Look! Mary is drawing a picture.	☐	☐
	....		
b)	Betty is just eating an apple.	☐	☐
	....		
c)	Mary is listening to music at the moment.	☐	☐
	....		
d)	Look! Bob and Peter are writing their homework.	☐	☐
	....		
e)	Just now, the dog is watching the boys.	☐	☐
	....		
f)	Anne is just writing a book.	☐	☐
	....		
g)	At the moment John and Anne are playing the guitar.	☐	☐
	....		
h)	Listen! A bird is singing.	☐	☐
	....		

REGEL

Im Englischen kommt das *present progressive* häufig mit bestimmten Wörtern vor, die darauf hinweisen, dass eine Handlung gerade abläuft.

Signalwörter:

- *just* – gerade
- *just now* – gerade jetzt
- *still* – immer noch
- *at the moment* – im Augenblick
- *Look!* – Schau!
- *Listen!* – Hör mal!

5 Can you underline the signal words in exercise 3?
Kannst du die Signalwörter in Aufgabe 3 unterstreichen?

Peter's Saturday

22

6 Listen to what Peter is doing on Saturday.
Find the right order of the pictures. Fill in the numbers from 1 to 6.
Höre dir an, was Peter diesen Samstag macht.
Bestimme die richtige Reihenfolge der Bilder und schreibe die Nummern 1 bis 6 in die Kästchen.

a)

b)

c)

d)

e)

f)

7 **Listen to the recording. Draw the hands and write down what the people are doing.**
Höre gut zu. Zeichne die fehlenden Zeiger ein und schreibe auf, was die Personen gerade machen.

23

a) At 

Peter .... breakfast.

His father .... a newspaper and his mother

.... tea.

b) At 

Peter .... to the radio.

c) At 

Peter .... still .... to the music, but he ....

.... a comic, too.

He is thirsty.

d) At 

Peter is in the kitchen. He ....

....

.... juice.

At that moment the phone

....

e) At 

Peter and John .... football outside. Two girls

.... them.

f) At 

Peter's family is at home. His parents

.... cards and Peter

.... TV.

Free time activities

8 Can you match the words with the activities?
Kannst du die Wörter mit den Aktivitäten verbinden?
Manchmal ist das nicht so schwer, weil viele englischen Wörter den deutschen Entsprechungen ähnlich sind.

fishing
playing tennis
doing judo
climbing
swimming
riding a bike
skiing
skating

24

9 Now listen and find out, who is doing what.
Tick the correct box.
Höre dir nun die Aufnahme an und finde heraus, wer was macht.
Kreuze das jeweils richtige Kästchen an.

	John	Bob	Anne	Peter	Mary	Betty
swimming	☐	☐	☐	☐	☐	☐
climbing	☐	☐	☐	☐	☐	☐
skating	☐	☐	☐	☐	☐	☐
skiing	☐	☐	☐	☐	☐	☐
riding a bike	☐	☐	☐	☐	☐	☐
doing judo	☐	☐	☐	☐	☐	☐
fishing	☐	☐	☐	☐	☐	☐

10 Can you make sentences now?
Kannst du nun Sätze bilden?

Beispiel: *John is riding his bike and he is doing judo.*

Bob ....

Anne ....

Peter ....

Mary ....

Betty ....

11 Read the short dialogue.
Lies den kurzen Dialog.

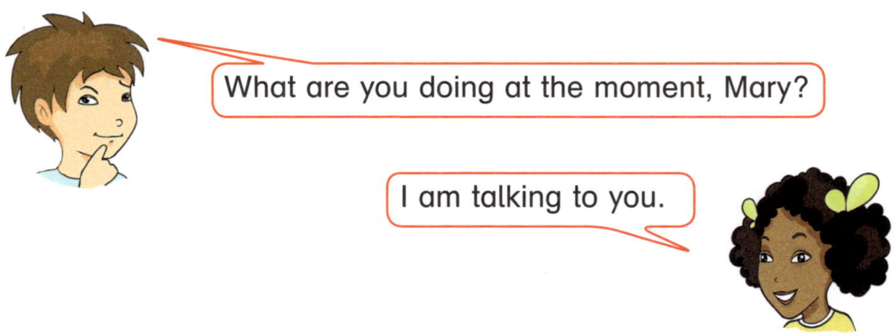

REGEL

Nicht vergessen:

Das *present progressive* wird in der **ersten Person Singular** mit *am* + *verb* + *-ing* gebildet. ***I am swimming.***

Das *present progressive* wird in der **zweiten Person Singular** mit *are* + *verb* + *-ing* gebildet. ***You are riding my bike.***

What about you? – Und du?

What are you doing at the moment?

I am ....

12 **Peter is talking to Mary on the phone.**
Put the verbs in brackets into the present progressive.
Peter telefoniert mit Mary.
Setze die Verben in Klammern ins *present progressive*
(= Verlaufsform der Gegenwart).

– Hello Mary! What are you doing at the moment?

– Hi Peter! Well, I .... (do) many things right now.

I .... (sit) on the floor and I .... (talk) to you on the phone. I .... (do) my homework and I .... (drink) a cup of tea.

– Wow! That's really a lot! What about John?

– John? He .... (listen) to some CDs with Bob.

Listen! They .... (make) a terrible noise and now Dusty, our neighbour's dog, ... (bark) at the boys. He thinks they .... (play) with him.

My poor parents. They .... (watch) TV, but now they can't hear anything because of the noise.

Hobbies

13 Which hobbies do you like? Which hobbies don't you like?
Welche Hobbys magst du? Welche magst du nicht?

I like / don't like swimming.

a) ……………………………………

b) ……………………………………

c) ……………………………………

d) ……………………………………

e) ……………………………………

f) ……………………………………

g) ……………………………………

h) ……………………………………

TIPP

Hast du dein Hobby nicht gefunden?
Versuche, es im Wörterbuch zu finden –
oder im Internet, z. B. bei: http://dict.tu-chemnitz.de/

Zwischentest

My free time

1 What is right? Tick it.
Was ist richtig? Kreuze an.

a)
☐ The boy is reading to the TV.
☐ The boy is watching TV.
☐ The boy is doing TV.

b)
☐ The girl is drawing.
☐ The girl is reading.
☐ The girl is writing.

c)
☐ The boy is tired.
☐ The boy is having tea.
☐ The boy is eating tea.

d)
☐ The girl is skating.
☐ The girl is fishing.
☐ The girl is climbing.

e) They
☐ is watching TV.
☐ am drawing a picture.
☐ are watching TV.

f) He
☐ am doing Judo.
☐ are climbing.
☐ is skiing.

g) You
☐ is skating.
☐ are playing basketball.
☐ is singing.

h) I
☐ are listening to the music.
☐ am reading a comic.
☐ is playing cards.

maximale Punktzahl 8

2 What is wrong? Tick it.
Was ist falsch? Kreuze an.

a) I am doing
☐ my homework.
☐ judo.
☐ a picture.

b) She is playing
☐ TV.
☐ computer games.
☐ the guitar.

maximale Punktzahl 2

Gesamtpunktzahl
.... von 10

Lernplaner

Kontrolliere deine Ergebnisse mithilfe der Lösungen (Seite 110) und addiere die erreichten Punkte.

☐ 10 bis 8 Punkte: ☺   ☐ 7 bis 5 Punkte: 😐   ☐ 4 bis 0 Punkte: ☹

The year

Das lernst du hier:

- ➡ Wie du die Feier- und Wochentage bezeichnest.
- ➡ Wie und wann du das *simple present* verwendest.

Holidays

1 **Write the words under the pictures.**
Schreibe die Wörter unter die Bilder.

a) Halloween words – Wörter zum Thema „Halloween“

witch · ghost · vampire · pumpkin · skeleton · spider

b) Christmas words – Wörter zum Thema „Weihnachten“

epersnt

singotck

ntSaa Calsu

einererd	naleg	chsrtatrismee
....	....	....

2 **Easter words. For these words you need a mirror. Write the words on the lines. Wörter zum Thema „Ostern". Für diese Wörter brauchst du einen Spiegel. Schreibe die Wörter auf die Zeilen.**

dmɒl	Eɒsʇǝɹ puuuʎ	ʇǝʞsɒq
....	....	....

ɓɓǝ ɹǝʇsɒƎ	ɥsnq	ʇlowǝɹs
....	....	....

TIPP

Auch die Weihnachtsbräuche in Großbritannien unterscheiden sich von unseren. Geschenke gibt es nicht an Heiligabend (*Christmas Eve*), sondern erst am Morgen des 25. Dezembers (*Christmas Day*). Damit der Weihnachtsmann auch die richtigen Geschenke in die großen Strümpfe (*stockings*) am Kamin (*fireplace*) legen kann, sind britische Kinder in den Tagen vor Weihnachten häufig damit beschäftigt, Wunschzettel zu schreiben, die sie dann zusammen mit einigen Leckereien für *Father Christmas* vor die Haustür oder auf den Kaminsims legen. In Häuser oder Wohnungen, die keinen richtigen offenen Kamin haben, gibt es dafür manchmal einen unechten Kaminvorbau.

Days of the week

3 Find out the right days of the week.
Trage die richtigen Wochentage ein.

May 22nd is a Monday.

a) May 28th is a .... b) May 26th is a ....
c) May 25th is a .... d) May 27th is a ....
e) May 24th is a .... f) May 23rd is a ....

4 Can you write down the days of the week in the right order?
Kannst du die Wochentage in der richtigen Reihenfolge aufschreiben?

weekdays
1. ....
2. ....
3. ....
4. ....
5. ....

weekend
6. ....
7. ....

TIPP

Wochentage, Monatsnamen und Feiertage schreibt man auch im Englischen immer groß:
Monday, Tuesday, Easter ...

5 Write down the missing days. Trage die fehlenden Wochentage ein.

the day before	today	the day after
....	Wednesday	....
Sunday	....	Tuesday
....	Saturday	....
Thursday	....	....

Bob's timetable

6 **Look at Bob's timetable and fill in the missing words.**
Schau dir Bobs Stundenplan an und ergänze die fehlenden Wörter.

	MON	TUE	WED	THU	FRI
8.45 am	Maths		PE	Maths	
9.30 am	Maths	Maths	PE	Maths	Art
	History	Maths	History	German	Maths
	Biology	German	Maths	PE	Biology
12.30 pm	Lunch break				
	Art	Biology	Maths	History	Biology
3.00 pm	Art	Biology	Art	History	German
3.45 pm			Art	PE	Maths

On .... school starts at 8.45 am and ends at 3.00 pm.

On .... school starts at 9.30 am and ends at 3.00 pm.

On .... and .... school starts at 8.45 am and ends at 3.45 pm.

On .... school starts at 9.30 am and ends at 3.45 pm.

On .... and .... there is no school. It is weekend.

REGEL

Wenn du ausdrücken willst, dass etwas **an einem bestimmten Tag** geschieht, sagst du: *on Monday – am Montag.*
Willst du ausdrücken, dass etwas **regelmäßig an einem bestimmten Tag** geschieht, sagst du: *on Mondays – montags (jeden Montag, an (allen) Montagen, immer am Montag).*

7 Can you match the sentences with the pictures?
Kannst du die Sätze mit den passenden Bildern verbinden?

a)

b)

c)

I go home at 4.00.

I have tea at 5 o'clock.

I get up at 7.15.

I go to school at 8.15.

I have breakfast at 7.45.

I have lunch at 12.30.

d)

e)

f)

8 Can you write sentences about your school day?
Kannst du Sätze über deinen Schultag schreiben? Achte besonders darauf, dass du möglichst keine Rechtschreibfehler machst.

a)

....
....

b)

....
....

c)

....
....

d)

....
....

Hobbies

9 Look at the pictures and fill in the missing words.
Schau dir die Bilder an und vervollständige den Lückentext.

What are your hobbies, Bob?

On Mondays I play tennis.

MON	TUE	WED	THU	FRI	SAT + SUN

On Tuesdays I play ....

On ....

....

....

On .... and ....

....

REGEL

Wenn man ausdrücken will, dass etwas eine **Gewohnheit** ist und es **immer wieder passiert**, dann benutzt man das ***simple present***.
Das *simple present* wird mit dem Infinitiv (Grundform) des Verbs gebildet: *On Mondays I play tennis.*
Nur in der **dritten Person Singular** (Einzahl) wird ein **-s** an das Verb gehängt:
School starts at 8.45.
Bob plays the guitar on Fridays.

TIPP

Merke: He, she, it – das „s“ muss mit!

10 Mary's week – Can you write sentences?
Sieh dir Marys Kalender an.
Beschreibe in ganzen Sätzen, was sie jede Woche macht.

	what	when
MONDAY	guitar lessons swimming	4 pm 6.30 pm
TUESDAY	basketball	5 pm
WEDNESDAY		
THURSDAY	basketball	5 pm
FRIDAY	meeting friends	after school, afternoon
SATURDAY	cinema day, watching films	4 pm

On Mondays Mary has got guitar lessons at 4 pm and ……………

……………

……………

……………

……………

……………

……………

……………

……………

……………

……………

REGEL

Endet ein Verb auf einem **Zischlaut**, so wird ein **-es** angehängt.
to watch – she watches, to catch – she catches

REGEL

Das *simple present* kommt häufig mit folgenden Signalwörtern vor:
often – oft, *sometimes* – manchmal, *always* – immer, *never* – nie,
usually – gewöhnlich, *Mondays/Tuesdays* … – montags/dienstags …

***Present progressive* bei gerade ablaufender Handlung:**

➜ *At the moment, Bob is playing tennis.*

***Simple present* bei gewohnheitsmäßiger Handlung:**

➜ *Peter never plays football.*

11 **Your turn: say when or how often you … .**
Du bist dran: Sage, wann oder wie oft du … .

a) … play tennis. b) … read a book.

c) … get up late. d) … go to school by bus.

e) … ride your bike. f) … listen to music.

12 **Simple present or present progressive?**

a) First underline all the signal words.
Unterstreiche zuerst alle Signalwörter.

b) Put the verbs in the right form.
Setze die Verben in der richtigen Form ein.

It's half past six, and Peter .... (get up) now.

He always .... (get up) at half past six. On Mondays

he often .... (go) to school by bike. At school he usually

.... (see) his friends.

Now, they .... (play) football and

they .... (talk) about the first lesson.

Sometimes they .... (listen) to music, too. It is eight o'clock

now and Peter .... (sit) in his classroom.

He .... (listen) to his teacher. It's an English

lesson. The teacher .... (talk) a lot.
How boring!

Zwischentest

1 Tick the correct answer.
Kreuze die richtige Antwort an.

a) ☐ pumpin
☐ pumpkin
☐ pampkin

b) ☐ rendeer
☐ reinder
☐ reindeer

c) ☐ whitch
☐ widch
☐ witch

d) ☐ ester bunny
☐ easter buny
☐ easter bunny

e) weekday:
☐ Tuesday
☐ Saturday
☐ Sunday

f) weekend:
☐ Friday
☐ Wednesday
☐ Sunday

g) ☐ On Monday I go fishing.
☐ In Monday I go fishing.
☐ At Monday I go fishing.

h) ☐ John play the guitar now.
☐ John is play the guitar.
☐ John often plays the guitar.

i) Mary
☐ sometimes plays tennis.
☐ is sometimes play tennis.
☐ play tennis now.

j) Peter
☐ never playing football.
☐ is never play football.
☐ never plays football.

Kontrolliere deine Ergebnisse mithilfe der Lösungen (Seite 111) und addiere die erreichten Punkte.

☐ 10 bis 8 Punkte: ☐ 7 bis 5 Punkte: ☐ 4 bis 0 Punkte:

Lernplaner

Gesamtpunktzahl
.... von 10

Abschlusstest

A At school

1 Write the sentences: questions and answers.
Schreibe die Fragen und Antworten auf die Linien.

a) Is this ....  ....

b) Is ....  ....

c) .... 

....

maximale Punktzahl 6

2 Write down the numbers. – Schreibe die Zahlen darunter.

13	52	77	100
....	....	....	....

maximale Punktzahl 4

3 Connect the sentences with the same meaning.
Verbinde die Sätze, die dasselbe bedeuten.

A	*Please be quiet.*
B	*How are you?*
C	*What's … in English/German?*
D	*Repeat the word/sentence.*
E	*May I go to the toilet, please?*
F	*Open your exercise book, please.*

1	Wie geht es Ihnen?
2	Seid bitte still.
3	Wiederhole das Wort/den Satz.
4	Was heißt … auf Englisch/Deutsch?
5	Schlagt bitte eure Hefte auf.
6	Darf ich bitte auf die Toilette gehen?

maximale Punktzahl 6

Gesamtpunktzahl
.... von 16

Lernplaner

Kontrolliere deine Ergebnisse mithilfe der Lösungen (Seite 112) und addiere die erreichten Punkte.

Teilbereich A: ☐ 16 bis 13 Punkte: ☺ ☐ 12 bis 8 Punkte: 😐 ☐ 7 bis 0 Punkte: ☹

B My wardrobe / Body and feelings

4 Write down the colour. – Schreibe die Farbe auf die Linie.

 ....

 ....

 ....

maximale Punktzahl 3

5 Can you answer the questions? – Kannst du die Fragen beantworten?

Is Mia's top orange? No, ...

Are her shoes blue? ....

Is her skirt green? ....

Is the scarf white and red? ....

maximale Punktzahl 4

6 Fill in the gaps. – Vervollständige die Sätze.

eleven years • name • 95583 • hair • yellow • Cambridge

Hello, my .... is Mia. I'm .... old.

I have brown .... My telephone number

is .... My favourite colour is ....

I live in ....

maximale Punktzahl 6

7 Tick the right answer. – Kreuze die richtige Antwort an.

a) 

☐ He is sad.
☐ He is happy.
☐ He is tired.

b) 

☐ She is happy.
☐ She is hungry.
☐ She is thirsty.

maximale Punktzahl 2

Kontrolliere deine Ergebnisse mithilfe der Lösungen (Seite 112) und addiere die erreichten Punkte.

Teilbereich B: ☐ 15 bis 12 Punkte: ☐ 11 bis 8 Punkte: ☐ 7 bis 0 Punkte:

Lernplaner

Gesamtpunktzahl .... von 15

Abschlusstest

C My family / At home / Food

8 **Tick the right answer. – Kreuze die richtige Antwort an.**

a) My mother's sister is my
- ☐ grandparents.
- ☐ grandmother.
- ☐ aunt.

b) How old is Oliver?
- ☐ His ten years old.
- ☐ He is ten years old.
- ☐ She is ten years old.

maximale Punktzahl 2

9 **Do you know this? – Erkennst du, worum es geht?**

a) You sleep on it at night. ....

b) You sit on it at the desk. ....

c) Your clothes are in it. ....

maximale Punktzahl 3

10 **Answer the questions. – Beantworte die Fragen.**

Do you like toast and eggs for breakfast?

☺ Yes, ...

Do you like pizza for dinner?

☹ ....

maximale Punktzahl 2

11 **Draw the hands. – Zeichne die Zeiger ein.**

a) 

It's eleven o'clock.

b) 

It's three o'clock.

c) 

It's nine o'clock.

maximale Punktzahl 3

Gesamtpunktzahl .... von 10

Lernplaner

Kontrolliere deine Ergebnisse mithilfe der Lösungen (Seite 112) und addiere die erreichten Punkte.

Teilbereich C: ☐ 10 bis 8 Punkte: ☺ ☐ 7 bis 5 Punkte: 😐 ☐ 4 bis 0 Punkte: ☹

Abschlusstest

D Nature / My spare time

12 **What do you see? Make sentences.**
Was siehst du? Bilde Sätze.

a) 
b) 
c) 
d) 

a) This is a ....
c) This ....
b) These are two ....
d) These are ....

maximale Punktzahl 4

13 **Make sentences.**
Bilde Sätze.

In sunny hot . it is and London	....
In cold it is and windy Belfast .	....

maximale Punktzahl 4

14 **What's right? Tick it.**
Was ist richtig? Kreuze an.

a) He
- ☐ am riding his bike.
- ☐ are riding her bike.
- ☐ is riding his bike.

b) He
- ☐ is climbing with his friend.
- ☐ are climbing with his friend.
- ☐ is skiing with their friend.

maximale Punktzahl 2

Kontrolliere deine Ergebnisse mithilfe der Lösungen (Seite 112) und addiere die erreichten Punkte.

Teilbereich D: ☐ 10 bis 8 Punkte: ☐ 7 bis 5 Punkte: ☐ 4 bis 0 Punkte:

Lernplaner

Gesamtpunktzahl
.... von 10

Abschlusstest

E The year

15 What belongs together? Connect it.
Was gehört zusammen? Verbinde.

Easter

Halloween

Christmas

whcit

....

Eersat bynun

....

sgctoikn

....

maximale Punktzahl 6

16 Look at the pictures and complete the sentences.
Sieh dir die Bilder an und vervollständige die Sätze.

every Tuesday	next Thursday	on Fridays

a) On ....Tuesdays.... I play ....

b) On ....

c) ....

maximale Punktzahl 5

17 Write down the missing days. – Trage die fehlenden Wochentage ein.

the day before	today	the day after
....	Wednesday	....
Sunday	....	....

maximale Punktzahl 4

Gesamtpunktzahl
.... von 15

Lernplaner

Kontrolliere deine Ergebnisse mithilfe der Lösungen (Seite 112) und addiere die erreichten Punkte.

Teilbereich E: ☐ 15 bis 12 Punkte: ☐ 11 bis 8 Punkte: ☐ 7 bis 0 Punkte:

Zur Bewertung der Tests:

Falls nicht in der Lösung anders angegeben, vergibst du pro Teilaufgabe einen Punkt – bzw. ziehst pro Fehler einen Punkt ab. Sind Beispiellösungen angegeben, so bewerte dich selbstkritisch. Sei vor allem beim Einstiegstest streng in der Bewertung: Er soll dir schließlich zeigen, wo du sinnvollerweise als Erstes üben solltest.

Einstiegstest, Seite 7 bis 11

1 a) This is an eraser.
b) Is this a pen?
c) Is this a sharpener?/
This is a sharpener.

2 eighteen, twenty-three, eighty-nine, thirty-four

3 A2, B1, C4, D3, E6, F5

4 white, blue, red

5 b) No, they aren't.
c) Yes, they are.
e) No, it isn't.

6 name, ten years, orange, 2843, London

7 a) She is tired.
b) He is thirsty.

8 a) grandmother
b) His birthday is in April.

9 floor, garage, chair, window, door, wall, carpet, desk

10 Yes, I like cornflakes with milk for breakfast.
No, I don't like toast with cheese for dinner.

11 a) It's two o'clock. b) It's five o'clock.

12 a) This is a lion.
b) These are two birds.
c) This is a sheep.
d) These are three cats.

13 In Dublin it is hot and sunny. (2 P.)
In Cambridge it is foggy and cold. (2 P.)

14 a) They are playing tennis.
b) He is climbing.

15 (je 2 P.)

Halloween ghost

Christmas reindeer

Easter lamb

16 On Tuesdays I play cards. (1 P.)
On Thursday I play football. (2 P.)
On Fridays I go swimming. (2 P.)

17 Monday, Tuesday, Wednesday
Friday, Saturday, Sunday

At school, Seite 12 bis 20

1

1. desk	2. board	3. eraser
4. pen	5. chair	6. ruler
7. book	8. workbook	
9. pencil	10. pencil case	

2 What's this? It's an eraser.
What's that? It's a pen.
What's this? It's an exercise book.
What's that? It's a ruler.
What's this? It's a book.
What's that? It's a pencil case.
What's this? It's a schoolbag.
What's that? It's a pencil.

3 Objects, which aren't called:
1. 
2. 
3. 

4 Possible answer/Beispiellösung:
a) Is this an eraser? Yes, it is.
Is this a pencil? No, it isn't.
Is this a book? No, it isn't.
b) No, it isn't.
It's a/an ...

5 Possible answer/Beispiellösung:
b) We are form 4c. We are 10 girls and 14 boys. Our school is in Augsburg. We can all speak English and German, too. Our English teacher is Mr Fischer. His favourite colour is blue.

6 Julia is fourteen.
Tom is eighteen.
Bob's dog is five.
Julia's cat is ten.
Tom's dog is three.
My grandmother is ninety.
There are twentyfive pupils in my class.

7 a) eleven
b) twelve
c) twenty-one
d) one hundred
e) six

8 one, seven, eight, twelve, thirteen, fifteen, twenty, twenty-two, thirty-one, forty-three, fifty-six, sixty-one, seventy-nine, eighty-three, ninety, one/a hundred

9 Numbers, which are called:
5553489; 919823; 349812;
753417; 983462

10 5 4 8 9 1 1; 2 7 3 6 8 6
11 19 21; 40 91 33

11 There are three exercise books.
There are four pens.
There are five rulers.
There are six erasers.
There are seven sharpeners.
There are two books.

12

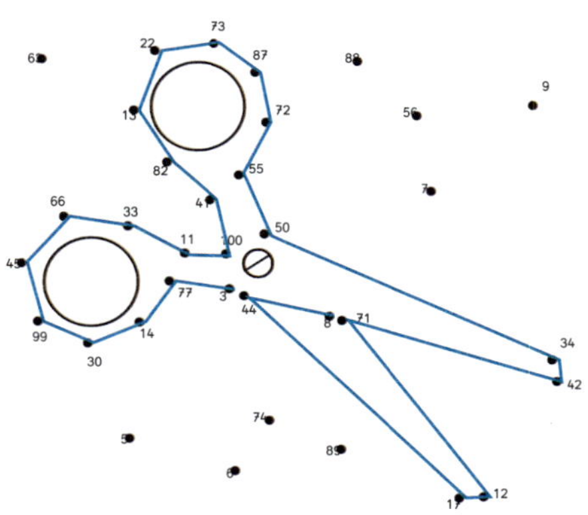

13 A2, B1, C4, D3, E6, F5, G8, H7, I10, J9, K12, L11, M14, N13, O15

Zwischentest, Seite 20

1 a) ruler
b) sharpener
c) pen
d) chair
e) eight
f) eleven
g) thirteen
h) fifteen
i) ninety
j) three

My wardrobe, Seite 21 bis 27

1 I'm yellow. I'm pink. I'm orange.
I'm black. I'm brown. I'm purple.
I'm green. I'm white. I'm grey.

2 1 Mary, 2 Anne, 3 Betty,
4 Peter, 5 Bob

3 Peter's balloon is red.
Anne's balloon is yellow.
Bob's balloon is orange.
Mary's balloon is green.
Betty's balloon is blue.
They are at a Halloween Party.

4 a) green and red b) grey
c) black and white

5 siehe Seite 103 unten

6 a) This is my black T-Shirt.
They are blue.
It is green and yellow.
It is red and grey.

7 Parts of the body: nose, finger, ear, knee, foot, eye, toe, arm
Clothes: shirt, pullover, trousers, T-shirt, jeans, skirt, socks, jacket
School things: eraser, ruler, book, desk, board, pencil, workbook
Colours: red, blue, black, grey, yellow, purple, pink, white

8 Susan:

Julia:

9 a) Susan's jacket is red and blue.
Susan's trousers aren't green they are grey.Her belt is brown and her shoes are blue.
Julia's T-shirt is pink with a red heart.
Julia's skirt is blue.
Julia's socks aren't red, they are grey.
The girls' shoes are blue.

10
1. This is Betty's book.
2. This is John's football.
3. These are the girls' shoes.
4. These are the boys' shirts.
5. This is Bob's hamster.
6. This is Anne's ruler.
7. These are the pupils' schoolbags.
8. This is Peter's dog.

Zwischentest, Seite 27

1
a) grey
b) blue
c) black and white
d) brown
e) This is a scarf.
f) These are boots.
g) This is a vest.
h) This is a green dress.
i) This is Betty's belt.
j) These are the girls' shoes.

Body and feelings, Seite 28 bis 34

1 knee, eye, head, toe, ear, shoulder, nose, arm

3 Hello, my name is Kim.
I'm nine years old.
I have black hair.
My telefone number is 12314.
My favourite colour is pink.
I live in Berlin.

4 Possible answer / Beispiellösung:
a) My name is Dimitri.
b) I live in Munich.
c) My telephone number is 985772.
d) I'm ten years old.
e) I have brown hair.
f) My favourite colour is green.
g) I like pizza.

5 Possible answer / Beispiellösung:
My name is Jacob. I am from Munich. I am eleven years old. My hobbies are playing the guitar and riding my bike. My favourite colour is orange. My best friend is Florian. I have got one sister and one brother. / I haven't got sisters or brothers.

6 My monster is green. My monster has got one head, three arms, three shoulders, no nose, five eyes, one mouth, one ear, black hair and four legs.

7 individuelle Lösung,
vergleiche Aufgabe 6

8 siehe Tabelle unten

10 Peter: “How are you?“
Bob: “I'm fine/happy. And you?“
Peter: “I'm sad.“

11 a) and b)

 Betty is tired.  Bob is fine.

 John is sad.  Anne is happy.

 Mary is hungry.  Peter is thirsty.

Zwischentest, Seite 34

1 a) knee b) eye
c) toe d) feet
e) hair f) shoulder

2 a) happy b) hungry
c) tired d) thirsty

My family, Seite 35 bis 46

1 b) grandfather: Paul 65 years
aunt: Sharon 31 years
uncle: Steve 25 years
mother: Meggie 30 years
father: Dan 30 years
sister: Mary 10 years
brother: Simon 5 years

2 Sharon is my mother's sister and my aunt.
She is 31 years old.
Steve is my and my brother's uncle and he is very funny.
These are my grandparents.
Eliza is my grandmother and Paul is my grandfather.
My parents are Meggie and Dan.
And this little boy is my brother. He is 5 (five) years old and his name is Simon.
He has got a cat family.

3 a) Die Lösungswörter sind:
sister, Großmutter, grandmother, Eltern, parents, Onkel, uncle, Vater, father, Bruder, brother, Großeltern, grandparents, Mutter, mother, Großvater, grandfather, Tante, aunt, Schwester (mit dem Wort sister beginnt die Aufgabe)
b) siehe a)

4 a) grandmother – Mia
b) kitten – Jo
c) grandfather – Oscar
d) mother – Mimi
e) father – Moritz

5 a) Possible answer/Beispiellösung:
This is Annie, the mother.
She is black.
She has got a red dress.
This is Mini, Maxi's sister.
She is black.
She has got a pink T-Shirt.
This is Maxi, Mini's brother.
He is brown.
He has got blue trousers.
b) individuelle Lösung, vergleiche Sätze von Teilaufgabe a)

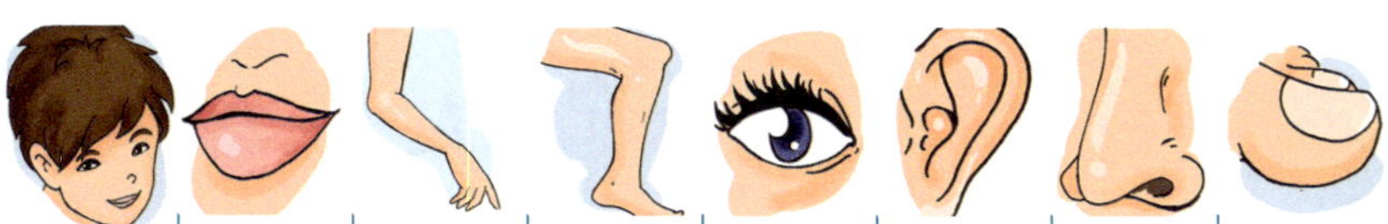

Betty	1	1	2	1	4	3	1	8
Peter	3	1	2	2	3	12	1	3
John	1	2	2		5		1	6
Anne	1	1			4	2		3
Mary	1		4	4	1	1	4	
Bob	2	2	6	5	1		8	7
Marc	3	2	4	7	1	4	1	10

6 brother – sister, uncle – aunt, father – mother, grandmother – grandfather, little – big, he – she, girl – boy, new – old, young – old

7 individuelle Lösung

8
a) Peter, 11 years, in September; Simon, 5 years, in December
b) Peter is Mary's friend. He is eleven years old. His birthday is in September.
Simon is Mary's little brother. He is five years old. His birthday is in December.

9 BIRTHDAY

10

11
a) for **his** birthday
b) **My** sister
c) **its** house
d) **her** room
e) **your** football, **his** wardrobe
f) **their** jackets, **their** schoolbags
g) **our** exercise books
h) **your** new car, **its** colour
i) **My** mother, **my** homework

Zwischentest, Seite 46

1
a) parents
b) uncle
c) grandfather
d) his grandfather
e) her uncle
f) My name is …
g) They are 10 years old.
h) He is 11 years old.
i) Her birthday is in August.
j) Their telephone number is 0432-236750.

At home, Seite 47 bis 55

1

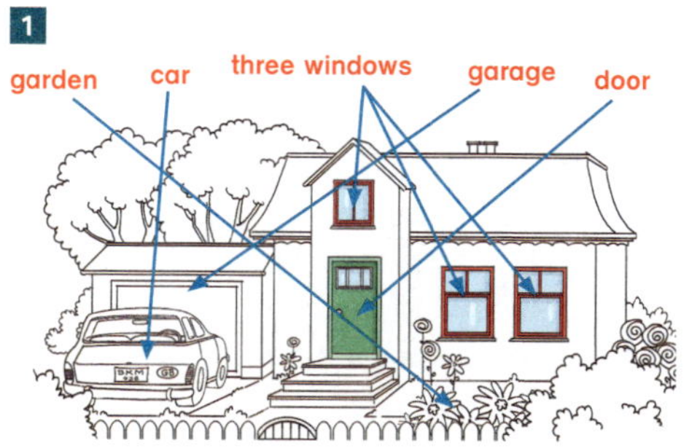

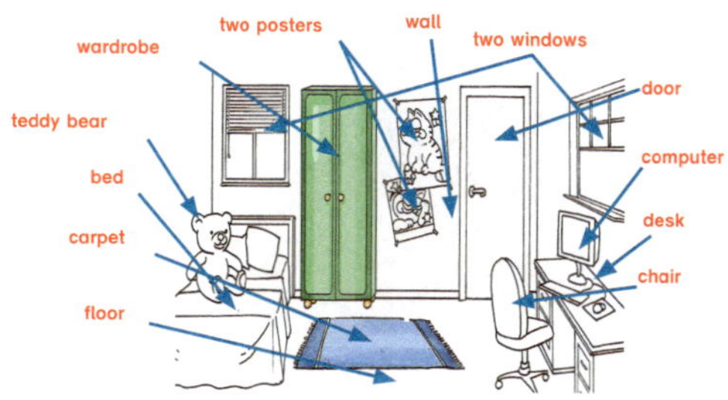

2 Bob's family has got a house with a garden. There is a garage for the car. The house has got three windows and a green door.
In Bob's room is a desk and a chair. The teddy bear is on the bed. And there is a wardrobe for the clothes. The blue carpet is on the floor. And there are two posters on the wall, too.

3 This is Bob's ~~house~~ home. His family has got a house with a ~~chair~~ garden and a ~~table~~ garage for the car. The ~~garden~~ house has got three red windows and a green ~~window~~ door.
This is Bob's room. The ~~house~~ room has got two big ~~doors~~ windows and under the right window is a ~~carpet~~ desk with a chair. On the desk is a ~~book~~ computer. In the room is a bed, too. There is a teddy bear on the ~~desk~~ bed. Next to the bed is a ~~chair~~ wardrobe for the clothes. It is green. And there is a blue ~~poster~~ carpet in the middle of the room on the ~~wall~~ floor.The door is to the right. Next to the door are two ~~books~~ posters on the ~~floor~~ wall. Bob is a big fan of Garfield!

4 The cat is under the chair.
The cat is next to the chair.
The cat is between the chairs.

5 The poster is on the wall.
There is a wardrobe in the room.
The teddy bear is on the chair.
The window is next to the door.
The clothes are next to the door.
The carpet is on the floor.
A coat is in the wardrobe.
The bed is under the window.
The cap is next to the coat.
The cars are under the bed.

6 The bed is red.

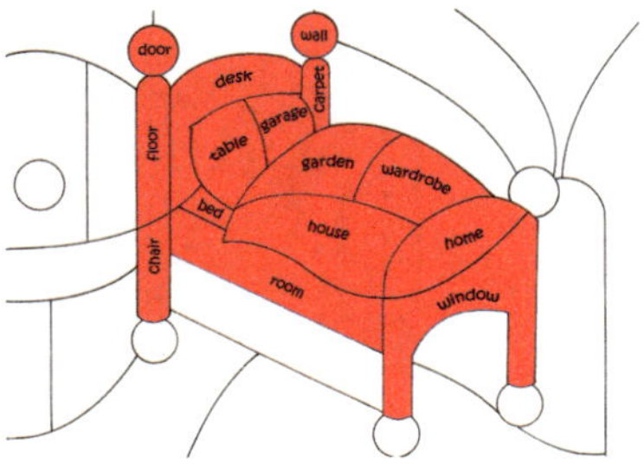

7 a) Picture 1:
The bed is under the poster.
The sweatshirt is in the wardrobe.
Picture 2:
The car is under the bed.
The wardrobe is next to the bed.
Picture 3:
The poster is on the wall.
The teddy bear is in the wardrobe.

b) Picture 1 – John
Picture 2 – Peter
Picture 3 – Anne

8 a) Individuelle Lösung, orientiere dich an den Beispielsätzen.
b) individuelle Lösung

9 a)

D	E	S	B	W	C	H	A	I	R
O	S	F	G	I	G	C	A	A	H
O	W	O	A	N	A	P	R	D	D
N	W	A	R	D	R	O	B	E	E
H	A	F	D	O	A	S	R	L	S
O	L	L	E	W	G	O	O	P	K
U	L	O	N	B	E	D	O	N	M
S	D	O	O	E	S	S	M	D	K
E	N	R	B	C	A	R	P	E	T

b) house, wall, floor, garden, window, garage, room, desk, chair, wardrobe, bed, carpet

10 Angekreuzt werden muss:
a wardrobe, a ball, one car, one poster, dresses, a window, a teddy bear, two shoes, a schoolbag, a book

11 Possible answer / Beispiellösung:
The teddy bear is on the bed.
Two shoes are under the bed.
The desk is under the window.
The schoolbag is next to the desk.
One book is on the desk.
The bed is next to the wardrobe.
The poster is on the wall.
The car is under the chair.
The ball is on the wardrobe.

12 b) Possible answer / Beispiellösung:
This is not Peter's house, because it has a small garage for one car and there are two trees in the garden. The big living room has got two doors. The small bathroom has got a window.

13 a) und b) individuelle Lösung, orientiere dich an den Beispielsätzen.

Zwischentest, Seite 55

1 a) This is a door.
b) This is a wardrobe.

2 a) car
b) poster
c) chair
d) and

3 a) The cat is under the table.
b) The cat is next to Tim.
c) The poster is on the wall next to the chair.
d) The bed is on the floor under the window.

Food and time, Seite 56 bis 66

2

3 I can see three bananas.
I can see one orange.
I can see five pears.
I can see eight cherries.
I can see six strawberries.
I can see nine lemons.
I can see four melons.
I can see two pineapples.

4 a) I like lemons. I don't like lemons.
b) I like bananas. I don't like bananas.
c) I like cherries. I don't like cherries.
d) I like pineapples.
I don't like pineapples.
e) I like pears. I don't like pears.
f) I like apples. I don't like apples.

5

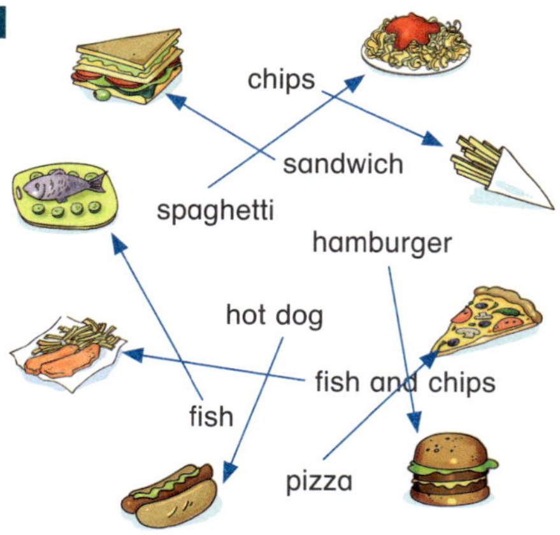

6 a) apples
b) cherries
c) lemons
d) drinks
e) strawberries
f) oranges
g) sandwiches
h) fish
h) pizzas
j) melons

7 hot dog, spaghetti, sandwich, fish and chips, hamburger, pizza

8 Breakfast: orange juice, tea, banana, pineapple, strawberry, cereal
Lunch/dinner: hot dog, tea, spaghetti, banana, pineapple, fish, chips, strawberry, hamburger, pizza

9

10 a) spaghetti b) cheese
c) cup d) banana e) milk

11

12 a) b)

c)

d) It's four o'clock.
e) It's six o'clock.
f) It's twelve o'clock.
g) It's eight o'clock.

13 Peter: "Do you like cereal and/with milk for breakfast?"
Betty: "Yes, I like cereal and/with milk for breakfast."
Peter: "Do you like toast and/with jam for dinner?"
Betty: "No, I don't like toast and/with jam for dinner.

Peter: "Do you like fish and chips for lunch?"
Betty: "Yes, I like fish and chips for lunch."

14 It's eight o'clock at Betty's house. Betty and Peter are hungry.
Everything is on the table for breakfast. There are two forks, two knives, two spoons, plates, cups and glasses. There is cereal and there is orange juice. Betty likes tea and cornflakes. Peter likes jam and toast with milk.

Zwischentest, Seite 66

1
a) pineapple
b) cherries
c) lemon
d) cereal
e) chips
f) tea

2
a) five o'clock.
b) two o'clock.
c) nine o'clock.
d) three o'clock.

Nature, Seite 67 bis 74

1

2
a) This is a dog.
This is a cat.
This is a sheep.
This is a rooster.
This is a hen.
This is a cow.
This is a pig.
This is a duck.
This is a horse.
b) These are three cats.
These are six ducks.
These are seven sheep.
These are four cows.
These are three dogs.
These are two roosters.
These are five hens.
These are two pigs.

3

4

5

M	E	I	U	O	E	R	R
O	C	A	T	Y	X	P	P
U	X	Y	W	G	B	H	H
S	R	A	B	B	I	T	H
E	F	W	T	T	R	L	H
L	I	Z	B	E	D	O	G
N	S	Z	I	E	I	U	O
L	H	A	M	S	T	E	R

6 The bird is on the table.
The dog is under the table.
The hamster is next to the book.
The fish is in the poster.
The rabbit is next to the desk.
The mouse is under the wardrobe.

7 "Weather words":
sun, sunny, sunshine, snow, snowing, rain, rainy, raining, cloud(s), cloudy, fog, foggy, wind, windy, storm, stormy, hot, cold, warm, shower, temperature, …

8 a) sunny, warm, cold, clouds, windy, shower
b) rainy, snow, temperature, foggy, sunshine

9 a) It is sunny. b) It is snowing.
c) It is windy. d) It is foggy.
e) It is raining. f) It is cloudy.
g) It is hot. h) It is cold.

10

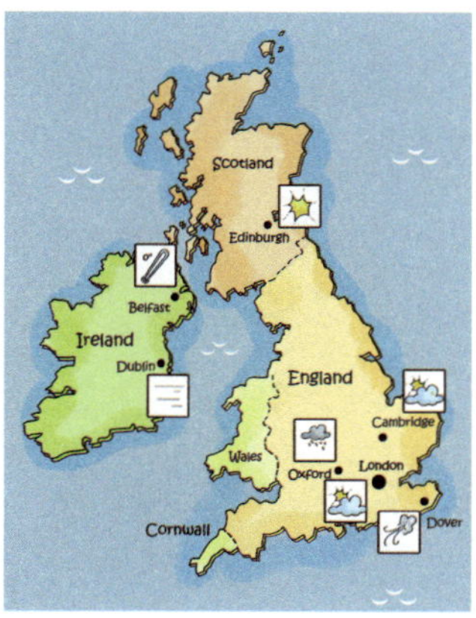

11 a) und b) individuelle Lösung

Zwischentest, Seite 74

1 a) cat b) sheep c) lion
d) monkey e) bird f) rabbit
g) mouse h) rooster i) It's sunny.
j) It's cold.

My free time, Seite 75 bis 86

2 a) John is reading a book.
Betty is drawing a picture.
Bob is writing his name.
b) Peter and Bob are playing cards.
Betty and Mary are having tea.
Anne and John are listening to a CD.
c) John is playing the guitar.
Peter is doing his homework.
Bob and John are watching TV.
d) Mary is eating a piece of toast.
Betty and Anne are singing a song.
Peter is drinking water.

3 John is playing the guitar.
Peter is drinking water.
Peter is doing his homework.
John is reading a book.
Bob is writing his name.
Mary is eating a piece of toast.
Bob and John are watching TV.
Anne and John are listening to a CD.

4 a) right
b) wrong: Betty is just eating a piece of toast.
c) right
d) wrong: Bob and Peter are playing football.
e) right
f) wrong: Anne is just reading a book.
g) wrong: At the moment John is playing the guitar.
h) right

5 zu unterstreichende Signalwörter:
a) Look b) just
c) at the moment d) Look
e) Just now f) just
g) At the moment h) Listen

6 a) 3 b) 2 c) 4
d) 6 e) 1 f) 5

7 a)

Peter is having breakfast. His father is reading the newspaper and his mother is having tea.

b)

Peter is listening to the radio.

c) Peter is still listening to the music, but he is reading a comic, too. He is thirsty.

d) Peter is in the kitchen. He is drinking orange juice. At that moment the phone is ringing.
e) Peter and John are playing football outside. Two girls are watching them.
f) Peter's family is at home. His parents are playing cards and Peter is watching TV.

8

9 swimming: Mary, Betty
climbing: Bob
skiing: Anne, Mary
riding a bike: John, Anne, Mary
doing judo: John, Bob, Peter
fishing: Anne

10 Bob is climbing and doing judo.
Anne is riding her bike, skiing and fishing.
Peter is doing judo.
Mary is swimming, skiing and riding her bike.
Betty is swimming.

12
– Hello Mary! What are you doing at the moment?
– Hi Peter! Well, I am doing many things right now. I am sitting on the floor and I am talking to you on the phone. I am doing my homework and I am drinking a cup of tea.
– Wow! That's really a lot! What about John?
– John? He is listening to some CDs with Bob. Listen! They are making a terrible noise and now Dusty, our neighbour's dog, is barking at the boys. He thinks they are playing with him. My poor parents. They are watching TV, but now they can't hear anything because of the noise.

13 Possible answer/Beispiellösung:
a) I like/don't like climbing
b) I like/don't like skiing.
c) I like/don't like riding a bike.
d) I like/don't like fishing.
e) I like/don't like playing tennis.
f) I like/don't like drawing pictures.
g) I like/don't like playing basketball.
h) I like/don't like reading books.

Zwischentest, Seite 86

1
a) The boy is watching TV.
b) The girl is drawing.
c) The boy is having tea.
d) The girl is climbing.
e) They are watching TV.
f) He is skiing.
g) You are playing basketball.
h) I am reading a comic.

2
a) falsch: I am doing a picture.
b) falsch: She is playing TV.

The year, Seite 87 bis 95

1 a) Halloween words: witch, ghost, pumpkin, spider, skeleton, vampire
b) Christmas words: present, stocking, Santa Claus, reindeer, angle, Christmas tree

2 Easter Words: lamb, Easter bunny, basket, Easter egg, bush, flowers

3 a) Sunday
b) Friday
c) Thursday
d) Saturday
e) Wednesday
f) Tuesday

4 1. Monday
2. Tuesday
3. Wednesday
4. Thursday
5. Friday
6. Saturday
7. Sunday

5 Tuesday – Wednesday – Thursday
Sunday – Monday – Tuesday
Friday – Saturday – Sunday
Thursday – Friday – Saturday

6 On Mondays school starts at 8.45 am and ends at 3.00 pm.
On Tuesdays school starts at 9.30 am and ends at 3.00 pm.
On Wednesdays and Thursdays school starts at 8.45 am and ends at 3.45 pm.
On Fridays school starts at 9.30 am and ends at 3.45 pm.
On Saturdays and Sundays there is no school. It is weekend.

7 a) I get up at 7.15.
b) I have breakfast at 7.45.
c) I go home at 4.00.
d) I have lunch at 12.30.
e) I go to school at 8.15
f) I have tea at 5 o'clock.

8 individuelle Lösung, vergleiche Aufgabe 7

9 On Tuesdays I play cards.
On Wednesdays I do judo.
On Thursdays I go swimming.
On Fridays I play the guitar.
On Saturdays and Sundays I play football.

10 Possible answer / Beispiellösung:
On Mondays Mary has got guitar lessons at 4 pm and she goes swimming at 6.30 pm. On Tuesdays and Thursdays she plays basketball at 5 pm. On Fridays after school she meets her friends. They have tea and play cards. Saturday is Mary's cinema day. They watch films at 4 pm.

11 Possible answer / Beispiellösung:
- On Mondays / Tuesdays / …
  I play tennis.
- I sometimes / never / often / …
  read a book.
- On Sundays / At the weekend / …
  I get up late.
- I never / always / …
  go to school by bus.
- I often / never / always / …
  ride my bike.
- I often / never / sometimes / … listen to music.

12 a) und b) It's half past six, and Peter is getting up now. He always gets up at half past six. On Monday he often goes to school by bike. At school he usually sees his friends.
Now, they are playing football and they are talking about the first lesson.
Sometimes they listen to music, too.
It is eight o'clock now and Peter is sitting in his classroom. He is listening to his teacher. It's an English lesson. The teacher is talking a lot. How boring!

Zwischentest, Seite 95

1 a) pumpkin
b) reindeer
c) witch
d) easter bunny
e) Tuesday
f) Sunday
g) On Monday I go fishing.
h) John often plays the guitar.
i) Mary sometimes plays tennis.
j) Peter never plays football.

Abschlusstest, Seite 96 bis 100

1 Possible answer / Beispiellösung:
a) Is this a chair? – Yes it is.
Is this a pen? – No, it isn't.
b) Is this a pencil? – Yes, it is.
Is this a ruler? – No, it isn't.
c) Is this an exercice book? – Yes, it is.
Is this a sharpener? – No, it isn't.

2 thirteen, fifty-two, seventy-seven, one / a hundred

3 A2, B1, C4, D3, E6, F5

4 yellow, green, pink

5 No, her top is yellow.
Yes, her shoes are blue.
No, her skirt is grey.
No, the scarf is grey and white.

6 name, eleven years, hair, 95583, yellow, Cambridge

7 a) He is sad.
b) She is hungry.

8 a) aunt
b) He is ten years old.

9 a) bed
b) chair
c) wardrobe

10 Yes, I like toast and eggs for breakfast.
No , I don't like pizza for dinner.

11 a)  b)  c) 

12 a) This is a cow.
d) These are two hamsters.
c) This is a pig.
d) These are two hens.

13 In London it is hot and sunny. (2 P.)
In Belfast it is windy and cold. (2 P.)

14 a) He is riding his bike.
b) He is climbing with his friend.

15

Halloween witch (2 P.)

Christmas stocking (2 P.)

Easter Easter bunny (2 P.)

16 On Tuesdays I play tennis. (1 P.)
On Thursday I go fishing. (2 P.)
On Fridays I do judo. (2 P.)

17 Tuesday, Wednesday, Thursday
Sunday, Monday, Tuesday